# SACRED
# GEOMETRY

HISTORY,
BELIEFS,
+ AND +
PRACTICES

# SACRED
# GEOMETRY

## AN A-Z REFERENCE GUIDE

MARILYN WALKER, PhD

**R**

ROCKRIDGE
PRESS

For general information on our other products and services or to obtain technical support, please contact our Customer Care Department within the United States at (866) 744-2665, or outside the United States at (510) 253-0500.

Rockridge Press publishes its books in a variety of electronic and print formats. Some content that appears in print may not be available in electronic books, and vice versa.

TRADEMARKS: Rockridge Press and the Rockridge Press logo are trademarks or registered trademarks of Callisto Media Inc. and/or its affiliates, in the United States and other countries, and may not be used without written permission. All other trademarks are the property of their respective owners. Rockridge Press is not associated with any product or vendor mentioned in this book.

Interior and Cover Designer: Tricia Jang
Art Producer: Tom Hood
Editor: Nicky Montalvo
Production Editor: Mia Moran

Photo credits: pages 156-157

ISBN: Print 978-1-64611-196-1
eBook 978-1-64611-197-8

R0

"EVERYTHING FOUND IN
THE EXTERNAL WORLD IS
FOUND INSIDE US AS WELL.
ONE COULD SAY THAT EACH
ONE OF US IS A MICROCOSM
OF THE UNIVERSE."[1]

—*Śri Mata Amritanandamayi Devi*

*This book is dedicated to the memory of* **CHARLES HUBBARD** *of Nova Scotia, a dowser and biodynamic farmer whose life was dedicated to honoring the Grand Design in all life, and to his dear friend* **SILVANA CASTILLO**, *also of Nova Scotia, who continues his explorations and teachings with love and dedication. May their wonder at Creation inspire us all to live the sacred in the everyday. Special thanks to* **TERRY MCKEOWN** *for a book he gave me years ago that I finally got around to reading.*

# CONTENTS

# INTRODUCTION

For centuries, the language of science has been mathematics with its subfield of geometry, which deals with shapes and figures and their relationships in space. Leonardo da Vinci's understanding of geometry and art revealed certain "roots," such as the Fibonacci sequence and the golden mean—basic languages found universally in nature and expressed in every culture. Albert Einstein viewed the world essentially as a geometrical structure. Today, diverse disciplines such as parapsychology and mythology, along with pioneering "new sciences" such as astrophysics, cosmology, and neuroscience, explore the underlying structure and order of the universe through geometry.

Recent research in the emerging field of consciousness studies suggests that mathematics actually supports the idea of the universe as conscious. Emerging mathematical models imply that everything, from an electron to the universe itself, has consciousness "in principle" and "lets you put a number on a system's degree of consciousness," from the simple forms of consciousness of an electron or other basic entity to more complex human consciousness—the former may combine to make the latter.[2] Although we don't understand what consciousness really is, Indigenous Peoples have known for millennia that a plant, a stone, water, a mountain, and so on, are sentient. Now, science and spirituality are coming together.[3]

Mathematics has been propelled incrementally throughout history, with one discovery making the next one possible. From the earliest discoveries in geometry to the most recent studies in consciousness, mathematics is evolving, as is the expanding universe it attempts to understand. Perhaps mathematics itself reveals each new layer of the mystery as our consciousness evolves to grasp it.

It has been quite a challenge to condense into a single volume what scientists and spiritual traditions have been occupied with for millennia. The content is not comprehensive—I have had to be very selective about what individuals, traditions, terms, and discoveries to include. And, even as the book goes to press, new theories arise about the structure, content, and purpose of the universe (of which there may be more than one).

Nature remains our greatest teacher and the ultimate source of mathematical and spiritual insights. By watching a bean plant grow upward, I came to understand chirality. In a tree's branches, I saw fractals, and in a nautilus shell, the golden mean; playing music taught me that sacred geometry is the root of musical harmony and rhythm. I hope the content, limited as it is, inspires each reader to delve further into the unfolding mystery to which sacred geometry holds the key.

# AL-KHWARIZMI

## (d. 850)

Islamic contributions to mathematics are many, as illustrated by the work of 9th-century Muslim mathematician and astronomer Muhammad ibn Musa al-Khwarizmi. The contributions of the vast Islamic empire (which incorporated mathematical developments from India and Greece) go back at least as far as 825 CE when al-Khwarizmi wrote his famous treatise. Translated into Latin as "algebra," it became the source of what we know today as algebra, whereby letters and other symbols are used to represent numbers and quantities in mathematical formulas and equations. Al-Khwarizmi is thus known as the "father of algebra" and, by some, as the "grandfather of computer science," for his development of the mathematical concept of the algorithm, a set of instructions or steps designed to perform a specific task in mathematics.

SEE ALSO: **Islamic Arts and Architecture**

# ANCIENT EGYPT

Among the first peoples to keep written records were the ancient Egyptians. Their earliest form of writing was hieroglyphics, which became the ancestor of most writing systems in use today. It was composed of about 1,000 distinct characters, many of which are recognizable pictures of what they represented. The implementation of a writing system meant that detailed records could be kept of complex designs for buildings

*Hieroglyphics from Medinet Habu, the mortuary temple of Ramesses III, in Luxor, Egypt.*

such as the pyramids; for canals and irrigation channels, which allowed for cultivation of land that was distant from water sources; and for water reservoirs in case of drought.[4]

The Egyptians expressed numbers according to a base-10 decimal number system. Using separate symbols for 1, 10, 100, 1,000, and so on, they would repeat each symbol as many times as the value it represented occurred in the number itself; for example, ∩∩IIII stood for 24.[5] Early hieroglyphic writings included the solutions of 84 specific problems in arithmetic and geometry, and Egyptian mathematics could calculate workers' wages, the area of fields for farming, and the volume of pyramids. So sophisticated was Egyptian mathematics that the Egyptian pyramid set the standard for what is generally recognized as the classic pyramid design: a massive stone monument with a square base and four smooth-sided triangular sides, rising to a point.[6]

SEE ALSO: **Square and Cube; Triangle and Pyramid**

# ARCHIMEDES

## (c. 287–c. 212 BCE)

Archimedes was a Greek mathematician, physicist, engineer, philosopher, astronomer, and inventor who is considered to be one of the greatest mathematicians of all time. Sometimes known as Archimedes's principle, the law of hydrostatics was supposedly made when Archimedes stepped into his bath, causing him to exclaim, "Eureka!" The principle states that a body immersed in fluid has an apparent loss in weight equal to the weight of the amount of fluid it displaces.

He is also credited with proving a range of geometrical propositions such as the area of a circle, the surface area and volume of a sphere, and the area under a parabola. Among his writings on geometry, mathematics, and mechanics was *Quadrature of the Parabola*, in which he documented his formula for a general parabolic arch and was thus able to determine the volume of an object with an irregular shape.

A widely known anecdote about Archimedes tells how he invented a method for using mirrors in warfare. Spinning a parabola around on its "nose," or point, produces a bowl-like shape called a paraboloid. This shape is used in mirrors and in such things as headlights, flashlights, and giant telescopes. Light, when it hits a parabolic mirror, bounces off and focuses on one spot, concentrating the energy of the light rays. By using mirrors as parabolic reflectors, Archimedes supposedly fought off Roman ships that were attacking his city; the mirrors focused light on the ships, causing them to catch on fire.

SEE ALSO: **Circle and Sphere; Parabola**

*Engraving of Archimedes (c. 287–c. 212 BCE).*

# AREA

Area is defined as the measure of a region enclosed on a plane (a two-dimensional surface).[7] The first known use of the term *area* was circa 1552, meaning "a level piece of ground."[8] The term seems simple enough for a general reader to understand, but how to calculate the area of different forms has challenged mathematicians for centuries, going back as far as the ancient Greeks, who developed formulas for calculating the surface area of simple shapes such as the square. For more complex shapes, mathematicians rely on advanced mathematics, such as calculus. As mathematics evolves to understand the structure of the universe, more and more secrets are revealed.

# ARISTOTLE
## (c. 384–c. 322 BCE)

*Aristotle.*

A Greek philosopher and scientist, Aristotle was a student of Plato's Academy in his early years. He authored around 200 works on astronomy, the earth sciences, and many other subjects, including the moral code of conduct needed for what he called "good living." He also taught science, mathematics, and philosophy. He is known for defining what he called the "golden mean": The ultimate goal of life, in his view, was living a moral life. This meant finding a middle ground between living deficiently and living to excess while considering the circumstances and needs of the individual. Such values were exhibited in mathematics: "The mathematical sciences particularly," he wrote, "exhibit order, symmetry, and limitation; and these are the greatest forms of the beautiful." He also considered, as described in Steven Scott Pither's *The Complete Book of Numbers*, "that truth, the axioms upon which mathematics is founded, were actual memories from the Spirit State before birth."[9]

SEE ALSO: **Golden Mean; Mathematics; Plato; Symmetry**

# ASTROLOGY

Astrology divines the supposed influence of the positions and aspects of the stars and planets on human affairs and events on earth. Interpretations of the heavens vary, but many cultures—from ancient Egypt to India, the Americas, China, and the West—have embraced astrology for a range of purposes, from predicting the future to explaining the past.

The Mayan calendar, for example, was used to identify when a particular event occurred or would occur in relation to other events and also determined when daily activities and rituals should take place for maximum benefit or to avoid evil influences. China's I Ching was used in medicine. Vedic astrology in India today might advise on the most advantageous place to live or the most auspicious time to marry.

Tibetan astrology calculates and interprets celestial phenomena by combining the Tibetan shamanic Bon tradition with Buddhism and Chinese influences. It shows, as described in *Tibetan Astronomy and Astrology*, "how one's life may be influenced by the planets and their movement, [by] one's past karma, or by beneficent or malevolent spirits."[10] Tibetan astrologers make use of the following numbers: five (for the five elements of wood, fire, earth, metal, and water), 12 (for the 12 animal signs), and nine (for the nine magic "square numbers"), as well as eight trigrams that come from China and are arranged in a circle around the nine. Their astrology also includes the Chinese yin/yang. Readings of one's life energy, health, financial situation, and success indicate where energy is imbalanced; antidotes will be prescribed to offset negative influences or prevent them from occurring in the future. In Tibetan culture, astrology and astronomy have been combined. In other places such as the West, astrology and astronomy are seen as separate and sometimes conflicting.

SEE ALSO: **Astronomy; I Ching; Shamanism**

# ASTRONOMY

Astronomy is the science of celestial objects and phenomena such as stars, comets, gases, galaxies, moons, cosmic dust, and planets, and of the physical universe as a whole. Geometry offers a way to contemplate the structure of the universe, to describe and ponder its origins and evolution, and also to measure it. Geometry, for example, calculates distances between objects such as planets and measures the speed and velocity of their orbits.

Among the many mathematicians and scientists throughout history who have contributed to the study of celestial geometry and our current understanding of the universe, two of the most influential are mentioned here. Seventeenth-century German astronomer and mathematician Johannes Kepler applied sacred geometry to astronomy to discover the laws of planetary motion; he did so using the Platonic solids as a model of the structure of the heavens. Albert Einstein's theory of general relativity led to what Elizabeth Landau has described as "the dawning of a new era of our understanding of the universe . . . [with] many important consequences for what we see in the cosmos and how we make discoveries in deep space today."[11]

SEE ALSO: **Kepler, Johannes; Music of the Spheres; Platonic Solids; Theory of Relativity**

# ATOM

In physics and chemistry, an atom is the smallest particle of properties retained by a chemical element. It is the basic building block of ordinary matter. Atoms are composed of subatomic particles called electrons, protons, and neutrons; the latter two make up the nucleus or center of the atom, while the electrons fly around the nucleus in a tiny cloud.

Approximately 99 percent of the human body is made up of atoms of hydrogen, carbon, nitrogen, and oxygen. Our cells are actually composed of particles that have existed for millions of millennia: Our hydrogen atoms were produced in the big bang; our carbon, nitrogen, and oxygen atoms were made in burning stars; and the very heavy elements in us were created in exploding stars.[12]

Molecular geometry, a field of geometry, investigates the three-dimensional structure or arrangement of atoms in a molecule. In simplified terms, such an arrangement determines how a molecule, as well as the compound it makes up, will act. Such geometries become the basis of all other forms from the human body to the entire universe.

# BEEHIVES AND HONEYCOMBS

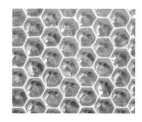

*Hexagon-shaped cells of a honeycomb.*

Honeycombs are precisely engineered storage units for nectar and larvae. The cells are prism-shaped with a hexagonal cross-section. The geometry of a hexagon allows for the most economical way to use the bees' labor and the wax the bees secrete. There exist only three regular shapes that could make up honeycombs of which the sides and angles are identical so that cells of identical size and shape pack closely together: squares, equilateral triangles, and hexagons. Of the three, cells in a six-sided hexagonal shape require the least overall wall length for a given area compared to the other two. The cell walls, made of wax, are an exact thickness and are gently tilted to prevent honey spills, and the comb is aligned with the magnetic field of earth.

A beehive is generally thought to be constructed through the process of self-organization, by which insects and other life-forms organize themselves rather than being influenced or ordered by an outside source. Some scientists suggest, however, that the soft wax of the cells might be pulled into shape by its surface tension in the same way that bubbles come together on a pond.

The basic overall dome shape of a beehive has inspired modular housing since ancient times as human architects and engineers try to replicate its properties.

SEE ALSO: **Area; Hexagon; Insects; Self-Organization; Square and Cube; Triangle and Pyramid**

# BINARY NUMBERS

In mathematics, the term *binary* is applied to a number system. Binary numbers are composed of only zeros and ones—they lack the numerals two, three, four, five, six, seven, eight, and nine. The number 1001100, for example, is a binary number. A "bit" is a single binary digit; thus, the preceding number has seven bits. Binary numbers, considered to be particularly beautiful because of their symmetry, are used for counting as an alternative to the commonly used base-10 decimal number system; computer technology uses binary digits. But as one mathematician put it, "There are 10 kinds of people in the world, those who understand binary numbers, and those who don't."[13]

| DECIMAL | BINARY |
|---------|--------|
| 0 | 000 |
| 1 | 001 |
| 2 | 010 |
| 3 | 011 |
| 4 | 100 |
| 5 | 101 |
| 6 | 110 |
| 7 | 111 |

*Equivalence table of decimal and binary numbers.*

SEE ALSO: **Symmetry**

# BIRD FLIGHT

Scientists studying bird flight incorporate mathematical models that measure the muscular, metabolic, and aerodynamic power in birds. U-shaped curves, for example, describe how birds' mechanical power varies with flight speed; however, the specific shapes and characteristic speeds of such curves vary depending on the bird's form and flight style. Though land-based movement is generally characterized by individual and separate steps, alterations in how a bird's wings move, as well as the impact of the air on flight speeds, make the changes gradual. Takeoff flight relates to the body size of a bird, but the mechanisms underlying such patterns are still to be discovered. Symmetry plays a role, however: Studies have shown that bilateral asymmetry is involved in the downstroke of the wings as a result of force produced in the chest area.[14]

Birds are also bilaterally symmetrical in their overall form, meaning that the left and right sides of their bodies can be divided down the midline to produce an almost exact mirror image of each other, providing balance which enhances flight. And studies have shown that symmetry is of benefit in mate selection: Female birds prefer more symmetrical mates because symmetry is an indicator of "good genes" and is associated with speed, strength, and fighting ability to protect the young. The offspring, too, will pass on such a preference.[15]

SEE ALSO: **Symmetry**

# BUDDHISM

Buddhism considers many numbers and geometric figures to have spiritual and esoteric significance. Such sacred symbols[16] provide practical instructions for liberation from the wheel of samsara (the endless cycle of life and death and of human suffering) and toward the ultimate attainment of enlightenment. They help one acquire insight into human nature and teach that spiritual awakening is possible. Such symbols are found everywhere in Buddhist communities—in homes and temples, on the street, and in other public places as well as in nature.

Sacred numbers—one, two, three, four, five, six, and eight—appear throughout Buddhist practices and instructions, such as the Four Noble Truths, the Eightfold Paths, and the Sacred Three also known as the Three Jewels: the Buddha (who attained enlightenment under a bodhi tree or "tree of awakening"), the Dharma or Cosmic Law, and the Sangha (or community of monks).

Two of the most important sacred objects of Tibetan Buddhism are the bell and the vajra, a ritual weapon. The bell represents wisdom, and the vajra represents method or purpose. Combined, they represent the union of all dualities—male/female, appearance/reality, and so on—and thus symbolize enlightenment and the incorruptible and indestructible truth.

*Tibetan Bon masked dancer entering the courtyard of the Menri Monastery in northern India; his dress shows the outward-directional swastika (2005).*

There are many sacred symbols of Buddhism. The triangle, for instance, appears in two forms: upright and inverted. The upright triangle represents the male principle and the unmanifested power of resurgence, whereas the inverted triangle represents the female principle and the power of creation. Overlaid, they produce the sacred six-pointed star, representing the union of male and female principles.

The swastika likewise takes two forms: spinning outward, or clockwise, and spinning inward, or anticlockwise. The former is an auspicious symbol that promotes prosperity and good luck, whereas the latter is considered inauspicious in Buddhism.

SEE ALSO: **Lotus; Mandala; Mantra; Triangle and Pyramid; Yantra**

## CADUCEUS

*Caduceus showing entwined snakes and wings.*

In Greek mythology, the caduceus wand or staff was carried by Hermes, messenger of the gods. It became the standard symbol for medicine long before the double-stranded DNA was discovered. Its original form was a branch (often olive) or rod ending in two shoots and decorated with flower garlands and ribbons. Later, the garlands developed into two snakes that entwined in opposite directions, their heads facing each other. The pair of wings attached above signify Hermes's speed. Today the caduceus has come to symbolize the physician and to represent medical skill throughout the world.

SEE ALSO: **DNA; Symmetry**

# CAPELLA

Among its positions of note in the night sky, Capella shines as the third brightest star in the northern celestial hemisphere. To the naked eye, it looks as if it is a single star, but Capella is actually a star system consisting of four stars in two pairs. The first pair of stars are large and bright and thought to be cooling and expanding on their way to becoming red giants—the name given to stars in a late phase of cosmic evolution. The second pair consists of two faint, small, and relatively cool red dwarfs.[17] In metaphysical terms, the relationship of these two contrasting pairs suggests the balance of opposites portrayed in so many traditions—for example, the yin/yang symbol, the equidistant cross of shamanism, the intersecting pairs of a mandala, or the geometry of a yantra. Together they illustrate the well-known axiom "as above, so below," meaning that we see the same patterns in the cosmos as on earth, interpreting them in our rituals and ceremonies according to our cultural lens.[18]

SEE ALSO: **Mandala; Shamanism; Yantra**

# CELL STRUCTURE AND FUNCTION

The word *cell* comes from both Old French and Latin words meaning "storeroom" or "chamber." In biology, cells are the smallest units of life; they contain the basic molecules of life, and they are the fundamental units of all known organisms. As such, they have been called the "building blocks of life" because they cooperate among themselves to construct large multicellular organisms that include humans and other animals.

Cells come in a variety of basic forms that produce particular cell shapes; these shapes generally seem to underlie cellular functions. This "shape-sensing" by cells is based on mechanisms of self-organization. Thus, cellular geometry is conveyed into spatial information that guides complex and diverse cellular functions. Armin Haupt and Nicolas Minc write: "Besides the cell-type-specific relevance of cell shape, an emergent concept is that both the regulation and the functional use of cell shape necessarily implicate geometry-sensing mechanisms."[19] A cell that divides symmetrically, for instance, must be able to locate its precise geometrical center before it can produce its characteristic form. So, if cells are cooperative, alive, shape-sensing, and self-regulating, are they conscious?

SEE ALSO: **Sacred Geometry; Self-Organization; Symmetry**

# CHAKRAS

Most readers will be familiar with the chakras of the human body, a system that derives from India but has become common in Western alternative medicine. In Tibetan cosmology, the seven chakras are psycho-physical centers that "represent the elementary structure and dimensionality of the universe"[20] from the deepest state of greatest materiality

and primordial forces to immaterial enlightened consciousness. Within each center lie all the latent, potential forms of
the universe, which link the microcosm to the macrocosm.
Each center is represented by a lotus flower, and each petal
corresponds to a sound as the base of a complex system that
integrates the material, physical world with the spiritual.

SEE ALSO: **Cosmology; Lotus**

# CHIRALITY

Nature is essentially asymmetric with respect to chirality,
which means "left- or right-handedness." The term applies on
all levels, from plants to human beings, from the subatomic
to the macroscopic. Mirror symmetry is generally absent in
nature, so most of nature's objects are *not* identical to their
mirror image, meaning they possess chirality. Chirality examples exist just about everywhere. The DNA double helix, for
example, is twisted so that a DNA molecule and its mirror
image are not superimposable. Simpler forms, such as a sphere
or triangle, that *are* identical to their mirror images are called
achiral. Thus, in some views, the universe is asymmetrical.[21]

In the everyday world, there is usually a preference for
left- or right-handedness, though science does not really
know why. Humans, for example, are structurally chiral—the
heart is positioned to the left of center in the body, the liver
to the right. Anywhere in the world, however, most humans
are right-handed in the same way that a majority of climbing plants exhibit right-handed twisting (with a significant

minority of humans and plants being "lefties" and some exhibiting randomness). It seems that at some early stage in the origins of life on earth, the earliest molecules to master the art of self-replication opted for a particular stereochemical profile and in so doing determined the entire—right-handed—course of evolution.[22]

SEE ALSO: **DNA; Symmetry**

# CHRISTIANITY

*The Holy Trinity is often portrayed as a triquetra.*

*Celtic Cross at a graveyard in Ireland.*

Christianity incorporates multiple examples of sacred geometry and of sacred numbers. Three examples are mentioned here: the Holy Trinity, the Celtic Cross, and the paintings from the Lindisfarne Gospels. The Holy Trinity represents one God in three persons: Father, Son, and Holy Spirit. A legend of the Celtic Cross has it that this style represents the conversion of Pagans in Ireland to Christianity; it combines the circular Pagan sun with the Christian cross of the crucifixion. One interpretation says that the cross, placed on top of the circle, represents the supremacy of Christ over the sun, which was central to Pagan spirituality. Today the Celtic Cross has become a more general symbol of Celtic identity. The Lindisfarne Gospels, based on the four Gospels in the Bible, are an illuminated manuscript created c. 700, in Old English and Latin, at Lindisfarne Priory on Lindisfarne, also called Holy Island (a tidal island off the northeast coast of England). They are considered to be the most spectacular manuscript to survive from Anglo-Saxon England.

*The Lindisfarne Gospels include five carpet pages, so-called because of their resemblance to carpets from the eastern Mediterranean.*

# CHURCHES

Churches, mosques, temples, tabernacles, and other religious structures are universal examples of geometric shapes, ratios, and proportions applied for a metaphysical purpose. The geometrical layout of churches, for example, suggests a journey. The journey is actual, as one physically moves through its places and areas. It is also symbolic, contemplative, and ritualized—a "journey of the soul," in Margaret Visser's terms: "Churches are laid out with a certain trajectory of the soul in mind . . . an ancient and intentional order."[23] And their orientation is always to the future—their tall spires, for example, connect us to the heavens and to the afterlife.

The famous Chartres Cathedral in Chartres, France, is among the best-known examples of how sacred geometry has been applied to architecture. It includes 44 stained-glass windows and a 12th-century labyrinth that is still in use today. The sacred geometry of such architecture was a visual contemplation of the universe's ordered, mathematical structure and a direct link to the Divine, the Creator, the architect of the universe, who, as Plato wrote, "practices eternal geometry."[24] Another example, the Hagia Sophia church in Istanbul, Turkey, was designed by a physicist and a mathematician as an experiment in linking geometry, the behavior of light, and religious and cosmological beliefs.[25]

SEE ALSO: **Numbers; Plato; Sacred Geometry**

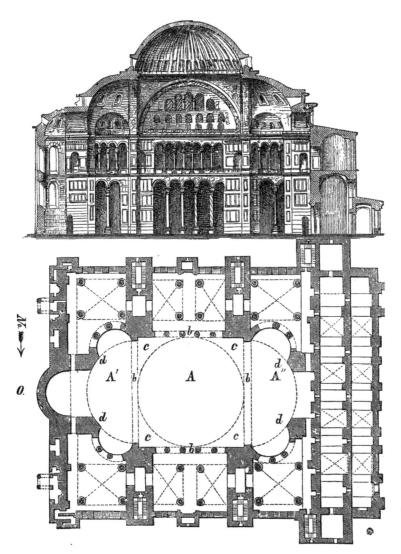

*This illustration of the Hagia Sophia church focuses on the geometry of the floor plan, the geometry of the apse, and light behavior in the original dome to reveal the structure's hitherto hidden design rules and features.*

# CIRCLE AND SPHERE

A circle is a geometrical curve made up of the set (a collection or combination in mathematical terms) of all points that are the same distance or radius from a given point or center. As such, it is a two-dimensional geometric form. In the natural world, a rainbow is part of a circle.[26] A sphere is a three-dimensional form of a circle. In nature, atoms, the earth, some seeds, and bubbles are spheres.

The circle motif is common in Indigenous arts, suggesting unity and wholeness. In the Circle Dance of Siberian Indigenous Peoples, each person can see and be seen by everyone else in the circle; leadership of the chant or dance emerges organically and spontaneously, and everyone is brought together in harmony and good will. The circle also manifests as the Circle of Life, which is the basis of Indigenous spirituality: Life and death are considered cyclical, one merging into the other such that the physical and spiritual realms exist in eternal relationship. It is also represented in the footprint of much traditional Indigenous architecture, as with the tipi or tent of First Nations and Native Americans, the Central Asian yurt or ger, the Tsaatan Reindeer Herder tent, and the Inuit snow house.[27]

As the basis of the First Nations and Native American medicine wheel, the circle is divided into four quadrants, which show movement and growth toward completion and rebirth through the four seasons (spring, summer, autumn, winter); the four stages of life (infancy, adolescence,

*Tents of the Tsaatan Reindeer Herders at summer camp, northern Mongolia, 2006.*

adulthood, elderhood); the four elements (earth, air, fire, water); and so on.

In Buddhism and Hinduism, the circle of the mandala points to the inseparability and interconnectedness of all existence; at its center is the awakened consciousness of our innermost being. But the circle is also the wheel of deluded existence or samsara—suffering and dissatisfaction. In this sense, the circle teaches that all that is gained in life is ultimately lost. Only the realization that this is a world of illusion is real and permanent.

A sphere is defined as the set of all points equidistant from a single point in space. It is thus a perfectly rounded, three-dimensional transformation of a two-dimensional circle. Bubbles formed on the surface of a pond or river are fascinating illustrations of the mathematical properties of a sphere: A bubble has the least surface area required to hold a given volume, thus requiring the least amount of energy to maintain itself. (The surface tension makes bubbles round.)

In spiritual terms, a sphere represents entirety or wholeness. Although it is one of the simplest forms in geometry, it can hold or contain all other geometrical shapes because all measurements are equal within a sphere.

SEE ALSO: Mandala; Medicine Wheel; Symmetry; Two-Dimensional and Three-Dimensional Geometry; Yurt

*Embroidered cloth from Siberia showing encompassing circle and its center point.*

# COSMOGENESIS

The cosmogenesis refers to the origin and development of the universe. When the universe became manifest, so did the original, primordial, and universal patterns, proportions, and relationships of what we call sacred geometry.

Countless cultures around the world from ancient times to the present celebrate and reimagine the cosmogenesis in stories, legends, songs and rhythms, carvings, paintings, and other practices through ritual and ceremony. Some innovate, perhaps receiving visions or instructions from the Spirit or the Divine. Others follow culturally specified patterns, insisting that rituals be followed exactly as they were expressed in the past, by the ancestors; they must be repeated without deviation. The cosmogonic structure is thereby preserved and honored, and the connection to human endeavors is renewed.

Mircea Eliade wrote: "Nothing better expresses the idea of creation, of making, building, constructing than the cosmogony. The cosmogonic myth serves as the paradigm, the exemplary model, for every kind of making. Nothing better ensures the success of any creation (a village, a house, a child) than the fact of copying it after the greatest of all creations, the cosmogony."[28]

SEE ALSO: **Golden Mean; Sacred Geometry; Symmetry**

*Embroideries by the Hill Tribes of Southeast Asia repeat these primordial geometries. As the maker re-stitches the patterns, often for clothing made for each new year's festivities, she recreates the original patterns of the cosmogenesis in a ritual of remembrance and renewal.*

# COSMOLOGY

A branch of astronomy, cosmology is the study of the physical origin and development or evolution of the universe—its past, present, and eventual fate. The leading scientific explanation for how the universe began is called the big bang theory, which, put in the simplest terms, says that the universe began with a singularity that then inflated over billions of years. Mathematical models and formulas are used to look back in time at the birth of the universe. From the big bang, which might be interpreted as "the One" or "the Source," came the diversity of life. Spiritual traditions have similar interpretations about the origins of the universe but use different terms. In Buddhism and Hinduism, for example, the sound "OM" is the universal sound of pure consciousness from which all sounds or vibrations emanated. These sounds formed the matter of the physical world in which we live. Matter, according to quantum physicist Michio Kaku, "consists of particles that are different modes of vibration."[29]

A recent theory, based on a 2016 find written about in *New Scientist*,[30] proposes that the big bang produced a "topsy-turvy universe" as well as our own, with the two existing in parallel. As Jon Cartwright writes, the "other" universe is a mirror of ours, where "positive is negative, left is right and time runs backwards" and everything is back to front and upside down. Most matter ended up in our universe, whereas most antimatter was channeled into the other one. Further, he reports, "this anti-universe would be contracting backwards in time towards the big bang rather than expanding away from it."[31] If this is true, it redefines physics as we know it and differs radically from our current view of cosmology but fits in with a view held by shamanic and other spiritual traditions that the universe itself (or universes) is composed of opposites.

SEE ALSO: **Astronomy; Shamanism**

## COSMOS

### SEE UNIVERSE (p. 125)

## CRICK, FRANCIS

### (1916–2004)

A world-renowned British neuroscientist and molecular biologist, Francis Crick is known for advancing the scientific study of human consciousness, which he explained at the neural level. Although he did not solve the mystery of consciousness, his pursuits contributed to the expanding interest in the science of consciousness. His 1994 book *The Astonishing Hypothesis: The Scientific Search for the Soul* remains in print today as a classic in the field.

Neuroscience studies the nervous system at different scales to reveal the underlying structure of a neuron, which is a cell of the nervous system. In an 1899 drawing by Santiago Ramón y Cajal, neurons are shown to be fractal.

Molecular biology developed as the study of gene structure and genetic inheritance. Along with James Watson, Crick is credited with first describing the geometrical structure of the DNA molecule as a double helix.

SEE ALSO: **DNA; Fractal; Helix; Molecule**

# CRYSTALS

In the 17th century, Johannes Kepler was interested in the shape of crystals—why was the shape so regular? But it wasn't until the 18th century that French priest and botanist René-Just Haüy discovered that crystal shapes are determined by the arrangement of the atoms that constitute them. Since the publication of Haüy's 1822 work *Traité de Cristallographie* crystallography, or the study of the crystalline state of matter, has been based on a direct space description of crystals.[32] Direct or crystal space describes the space in which the structures of finite real crystals are idealized as infinite, perfect three-dimensional structures.

Crystals are made as atoms stack three-dimensionally, producing "facets rather like the triangular faces of an ancient pyramid," as Philip Ball describes them.[33] They do so according to only seven simple geometric shapes that geologists call orders, with just a single change distinguishing one order from another. These orders range from the simplest cubic crystal, such as table salt, to the most complex hexagonal crystals, such as semiprecious tourmaline. Metals are among the simplest of crystals, since the atoms of which they are constituted are identical in size and so pack together efficiently, creating a dense structure.

Atoms in crystals also exhibit elements of symmetry, such as rotation or translation, which determine shape and relate to physical properties.

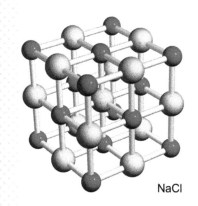

NaCl

*Isolated 3D model of a crystal lattice of salt.*

SEE ALSO: **Atom; Kepler, Johannes; Snowflakes and Snow Crystals; Square and Cube; Symmetry**

# CYMATICS

Cymatics is the study of wave phenomena. It was pioneered by 20th-century Swiss physician Hans Jenny, whose experiments used audible sound to excite pastes, powders, and liquids into lifelike, flowing forms that reflect patterns found in nature and in art and architecture. Such patterns illustrate how matter inherently responds to sound and how all life is part of an intricate vibrational matrix that has been called the "music of the spheres."

> "Our world is permeated throughout by waves and vibrations. When we hear, waves travelling through the air impinge on our ears. When we speak, we ourselves generate air waves with our larynx. When we turn on our radios and televisions, we are utilizing a waveband. We talk about electric waves and we are all familiar with waves of light. In an earthquake, the whole earth vibrates and seismic waves are produced. There are even whole stars which pulsate in a regular rhythm.
>
> "But it is not only the world we live in that is in a state of vibration . . . for our body itself is penetrated by vibrations. Our blood pulses through us in waves. We can hear the beat of the heart. And above all our muscles go into a state of vibration when we move them."[34]
>
> —Hans Jenny, "Cymatics: The Sculpture of Vibrations"

SEE ALSO: **Music of the Spheres; Plato; Pythagoras**

# DA VINCI, LEONARDO
## (1452–1519)

Scientist, artist, philosopher, and inventive genius, Leonardo da Vinci is universally celebrated for his accomplishments. There is so much to note about his life and work, it would take volumes to cover it all.[35] Of his many pieces and accomplishments, *Vitruvian Man*, the *Mona Lisa*, and his geometric drawings best illustrate his profound understanding of the link between humans and nature and of how sacred geometry permeates all life. Da Vinci believed in God, although he was at odds with the Christian doctrine of the time. Instead, his God, as Serge Bramly describes it, was "in the miraculous beauty of light, in the harmonious movement of the planets, in the intricate arrangement of muscles and nerves inside the body, and in that inexpressible masterpiece the human soul."[36]

Da Vinci's *Vitruvian Man* was created around the year 1487. Accompanied by notes based on the work of a famed architect of the time, it shows a male figure in two superimposed positions with his arms and legs shown apart and inscribed within a circle and square. The drawing and text are sometimes called the Canon of Proportions or, occasionally, the Proportions of Man. The universality of the design is reflected in the proportional relationship of the parts, while a stable structure is ensured by the equilibrium of elements.

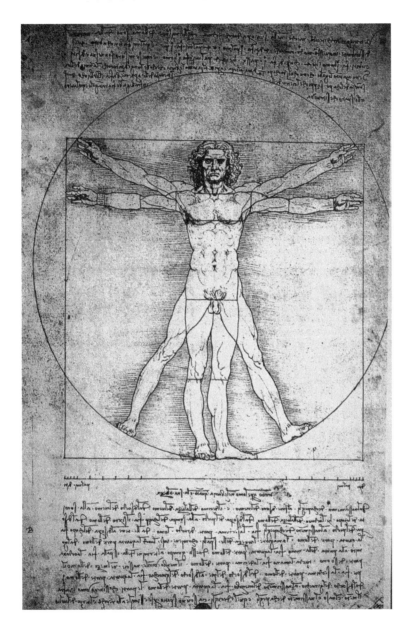

*Da Vinci's* Vitruvian Man.

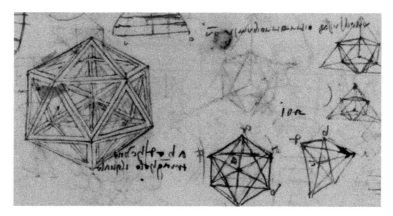

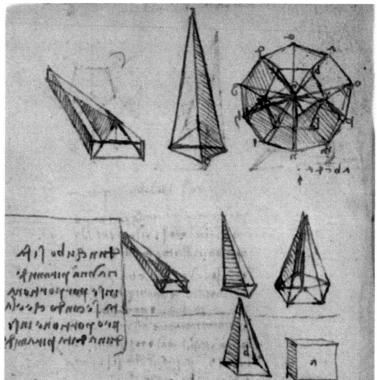

*Illustrations from* The Divine Proportion.

Such properties are shared by the human body as God's creation and a good building produced by human effort.

This architectural application represents the beginning of concepts with universal application. The idea of the artistic microcosm became one of the unifying principles of da Vinci's thought.[37]

Various artists and scientists have shown the composition of the *Mona Lisa* to be based on the golden mean. The structure produces a sense of harmony in the viewer and reflects the idea of an essential link connecting humanity and nature. As expressed in da Vinci's own words: "Nature is the source of all true knowledge. She has her own logic, her own laws, she has no effect without cause nor invention without necessity."[38]

> *"The divine character of painting means that the mind of the painter is transformed into an image of the mind of God."[39]*
> —Leonardo da Vinci

*Da Vinci's* Mona Lisa.

The book *De Divina Proportione* (*The Divine Proportion*) by Luca Pacioli, a contemporary of da Vinci's, was first published in 1509. Pacioli writes of artistic and mathematical proportion, particularly of the golden ratio or golden mean, and its applications to art and architecture. The book's woodcuts are taken from da Vinci's illustrations of three-dimensional geometric solids. The original manuscript may be viewed online.[40]

SEE ALSO: **Circle and Sphere; Golden Mean; Square and Cube**

# DIMENSION

In general terms, dimension refers to the size—length, width, and height—of an object. In mathematics, however, the term refers to one-dimensional objects such as a line or curve, to two-dimensional things such as a plane or the earth's surface, or to three-dimensional space. In physics and mathematics, it is extended to spaces of higher dimensions such as four-dimensional space-time and even to infinite-dimensional spaces. Benoit Mandelbrot, known for the term *fractal*, applied fractional dimensions to applied mathematics.[41]

SEE ALSO: Fractal; Mandelbrot, Benoit; Two-Dimensional and Three-Dimensional Geometry

# DNA

DNA is the abbreviation for deoxyribonucleic acid, which is present in almost all living organisms as the carrier of genetic information. DNA molecules are packaged into threadlike structures called chromosomes, which are self-replicating structures within cells. Chromosomes are found in the nucleus of living cells; the genetic information they carry is in the form of genes, which are segments of DNA. Simply put, DNA is in genes, and genes are on chromosomes.

A DNA molecule is in the form of a double helix—that is, two long, thin strands that twist around each other like a spiral staircase. The double helix structure allows for stability and prevents the DNA from being easily destroyed. Scientists point out that the structural and physical properties of DNA are closely related to its geometry and to its topology[42] (the way the two complementary single strands are intertwined).

SEE ALSO: **Cell Structure and Function; Helix; Topology**

# DUALITY AND DUALISM

In mathematics, the principle of duality applies to a branch of algebra, as described by William Hosch, "whereby one true statement can be obtained from another by merely inter-changing two words" as, for example, in the statements "Two points determine a line" and "Two lines determine a point."[43]

In a different sense, many Indigenous cultures have based their spirituality on the idea of dualism, or the idea that two basic categories of ideas, objects, or principles exist in the universe and that each exists in relationship with the other, its opposite. Heaven/earth, night/day, male/female, good/evil, and sun/moon are examples of such dualities. Further, such related but opposing forces or elements must be kept in balance with one another for the universe to operate as it should.[44]

SEE ALSO: **Mathematics**

# EASTERN MYSTICISM AND PHYSICS

Ancient Eastern scientists and philosophers predated modern physics and the theory of relativity in understanding that, as described by Fritjof Capra, "our notions of geometry are not absolute and unchangeable properties of nature, but intellectual constructions" related to particular states of consciousness.[45] Meditation, for example, allows the practitioner to go beyond conventional notions of space, time, and other experiences of consciousness in much the same way as does modern physics, which discovered that all time and space measurements are relative rather than being absolute truths. In Eastern mysticism, then, all intellectual concepts such as space, time, and identity are relative, limited, and illusory.

SEE ALSO: **Buddhism; Hinduism; Theory of Relativity**

# EINSTEIN, ALBERT

## SEE THEORY OF RELATIVITY (p. 117)

# ELLIPSE

In general terms, an ellipse is an oval or a closed curved shape that is flat. In scientific terms, it is a closed plane curve generated by a point moving in such a way that the sums of its distances from two fixed points are a constant.[46] By applying geometry to astronomy, Johannes Kepler discovered that the planets move in ellipses around the sun, thus expanding mathematics to the cosmic, macro level.

SEE ALSO: **Kepler, Johannes; Mathematics**

# EQUINOX

In astronomy, the equinox—either spring (also called vernal) or autumnal—occurs twice yearly. The term comes from the Latin meaning "equal night," in reference to either of these two occasions when day and night are of equal length because the sun is directly above the equator. Thus, twice a year, the sun illuminates equally the northern and southern hemispheres. Equinox also refers to either of the two points in the sky where the annual pathway of the sun intersects with the celestial equator, producing almost equal hours of daylight and darkness.

SEE ALSO: **Astronomy**

# EUCLID

## (born c. 365 BCE)

Euclidean geometry is a mathematical system attributed to the Greek mathematician Euclid, who became known as the "father of geometry." His system deals with points, lines, and planes and how they interact to form complex figures.

*Elements*, his textbook on geometry, has survived for more than 2,000 years and has become the basis for much of modern mathematics, such as analytical geometry and curved space-time. According to David Berlinski, Euclid brought together scattered propositions of geometry "to create a world in which there is growth, and form, and intimate dependencies among parts."[47]

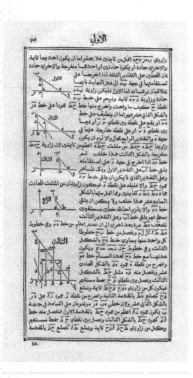

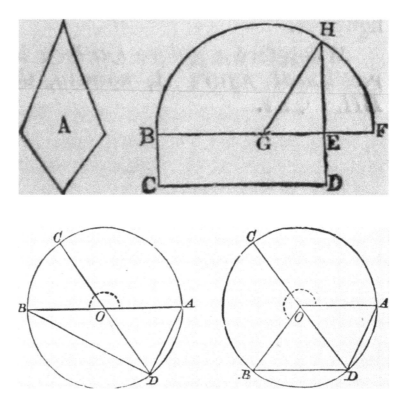

*A page and illustrations from Euclid's* Element.

SEE ALSO: **Geometry; Mathematics**

# FENG SHUI

Feng shui uses sacred geometry to locate buildings—especially tombs, graves, and temples as well as houses and other structures—and align them with the cardinal directions at places of power to provide them with maximum beneficial energy, or ch'i. It is used to locate what is called the "dragon vein," or ch'i channel: Where such veins meet, ch'i accumulates and becomes a power spot and optimum location.

Ch'i is the mysterious force, sometimes called the "cosmic breath," that is believed to be the vital energy of the universe. It exists in the heavens and in the earth as well as in humans and all other forms of life. Like all of nature, ch'i passes through the cycle of life from birth, to becoming strong, and to decay and death.

> *"Feng shui says that the opportunities come when the environment is right. Feng shui is the art and science of making the energy environment so supportive that one's attitude, opportunities, and luck change for the better."*[48]
> —Stephen Skinner, *Guide to Feng Shui*

Wind and water carry ch'i energy. If the energy in water, transported in streams, rivers, and so on, flows toward a site, energy can accumulate there. On the other hand, water flowing away from a building will lower the prosperity of the occupants, and stagnant water will cause ill health. The movement of ch'i, however, is affected by its source, by the direction from which it comes, and by the alignment of buildings and streets as well as by the arrangement of interior spaces. Beneficial ch'i in water does not flow too quickly, nor does it flow in a straight line that can cause it to gather speed and become dangerous.

Feng shui is not considered to be a religion or a spiritual practice, although its roots lie in China's religions of Confucianism, Buddhism, and Taoism. Instead, it is a set of practical techniques to manipulate ch'i in order to improve such things as wealth and prosperity, career prospects, success at school or in business, family cohesion and social life, health, luck, and so on.

Feng shui has been practiced in China for at least 2,600 years and possibly as far back as 6,000 years ago. With the Cultural Revolution in China between 1966 and 1976, traditional Chinese culture was discredited—buildings, libraries, art, and also feng shui paraphernalia were destroyed, and many feng shui practitioners fled to establish themselves overseas. Then, in the late 1980s, feng shui underwent a revival in China. Today, there exist many schools of feng shui, including variants that have developed in the West over some 45 years or so.

*Feng shui building in Hong Kong (Hong Kong Island).*

## FIBONACCI SEQUENCE

Fibonacci was the nickname of Leonardo of Pisa, a 13th-century Italian mathematician who revived ancient mathematics and contributed his own findings to the history of mathematics, including introducing the use of Arabic numerals (0, 1, 2, 3, 4, 5, 6, 7, 8, and 9) into Europe. Some of his work was based on the mathematics of Euclid. He is best remembered for what has come to be known as the Fibonacci numbers, or the Fibonacci sequence, which he developed in answer to this question:

*"A certain man put a pair of rabbits in a place surrounded on all sides by a wall. How many pairs of rabbits can be produced from that pair in a year if it is supposed that every month each pair begets a new pair which from the second month on becomes productive?"*

The resulting sequence is 1, 1, 2, 3, 5, 8, 13, 21, 34, 55, . . . [49]

The Fibonacci sequence is a numerical sequence in which each number is a total of the previous two numbers. It appears now in many areas of mathematics and science and, of course, in the natural world and is associated with the golden mean.

The Fibonacci Association, incorporated in 1963, focuses on Fibonacci numbers and related mathematics. It emphasizes new results, challenging problems, and new proofs of old ideas through publications and conferences, building on the discoveries of more than three quarters of a millennium ago.

Extending the sequence to 0, 1, 1, 2, 3, 5, 8, 13, 21, 34, 55, 89, 144, 233, the Fibonacci sequence appears in plants in their paired spirals that generally have particular values, in leaf arrangements of the majority of plants, and in the number of petals on many flowers, as shown in the following charts (pages 40-41). Variations and exceptions occur because evolution produces small but frequent changes in nature's forms.

## SPIRALS [50]

| | |
|---|---|
| Pinecones | 3/5, 5/8, or 8/13 |
| Smaller sunflowers | 21/34 (each going in opposite directions) |
| Very large sunflowers | 144/233 (each going in opposite directions) |

## LEAF ARRANGEMENTS: [51]
Estimated that 90 percent of all plants exhibit a Fibonacci sequence in their leaf pattern

| | |
|---|---|
| Elm, linden, lime, grasses | 1/2 |
| Beech, hazel, grasses, blackberry | 1/3 |
| Oak, cherry, apple, holly, plum | 2/5 |
| Poplar, rose, pear, willow | 3/8 |
| Pussy willow, almond | 5/13 |

## PETALS ON FLOWERS [52]

| | |
|---|---|
| White calla lily | 1 petal |
| Lily, iris | 3 petals |
| Buttercup, wild rose, larkspur, columbine | 5 petals |
| Delphinium | 8 petals |
| Ragwort, corn, marigold | 13 petals |
| Aster, black-eyed Susan, chicory | 21 petals |
| Plantain, pyrethrum | 34 petals |
| Michaelmas daisy, the Asteraceae family | 55, 89 petals |

SEE ALSO: **Euclid; Golden Mean; Spiral; Symmetry**

# FLOWER OF LIFE

Leonardo da Vinci is celebrated for his drawings of a geometrical structure that today is called the "Flower of Life." It has become a symbol of New Age spiritual growth and awakening but exists in many religions and spiritual traditions as an archetypal pattern of which many flowers, such as the chrysanthemum, are constructed. A geometric matrix that forms a mandala and a fractal pattern, its center represents creation or the source of life. Its interlaced circles of petal shapes show the symmetry by which the universe is organized and also portray the sacred vesica piscis, which represents the union of opposites. A flower, in many traditions, symbolizes both the impermanence and fragility of life and the cyclical nature of existence. For da Vinci, the Flower of Life encompassed the five Platonic solids, pi, and the golden mean.

*One of Leonardo da Vinci's drawings and modern renderings of a "Flower of Life."*

SEE ALSO: **da Vinci, Leonardo; Golden Mean; Mandala; Pi; Platonic Solids; Vesica Piscis**

# FRACTAL

The term *fractal* comes from the Latin word *fractus*, meaning "broken." Two principles are central to fractals: If any detail of a pattern is enlarged, the full design will emerge from it. And differences in scale do not alter anything about the pattern. These occur because a fractal is self-similar; that is, it is a structure that repeats itself at smaller and smaller, or at larger and larger, scales.

Fractal geometry, the "geometry of nature," is generally attributed to 20th-century mathematician Benoit Mandelbrot. Although some contest this, he is credited with coining the term to describe phenomena such as coastlines, snowflakes, mountains, and trees whose patterns repeat themselves.

> *"To see a world in a grain of sand*
> *And a heaven in a wildflower,*
> *Hold infinity in the palm of your hand*
> *And eternity in an hour."*[53]
>
> —William Blake, *Auguries of Innocence*

If we look at an aerial photograph of, say, a jagged coastline without using a measuring device, it's not possible to tell the length of the coastline—it could measure one mile or ten. As described by Philip Ball, "This indistinguishable appearance at different scales of magnification is a property called fractal . . . the fractal property discloses a kind of 'hidden logic' to the pattern,"[54] a pattern that is very common in nature and that belies the often seemingly disorderly arrangement of nature. The branching of a tree, as the stem becomes smaller and smaller, is a different pattern than the regular symmetry of a honeycomb, but it is no less pleasing as we seem to connect in some profound way to its hidden logic and its underlying simplicity.

The human body exhibits fractals, as in the fractal branching of lungs.[55] Our heartbeats are also fractal—and the more fractal they are, the healthier they are.[56]

Human-based art and design may exhibit an underlying fractal nature that is not at first recognizable as such but that almost subconsciously mimics the fractal geometry of nature. Pitch fluctuation and rhythm in classical music, for example, have a fractal nature. Fractals exist in literature as well—for example, in stream of consciousness writing such as James Joyce's *Finnegans Wake*, which has been associated with fractals of fractals, or multifractals. Jackson Pollock's drip paintings have also been studied as fractal, becoming more and more so as he aged.[57]

SEE ALSO: **Mandelbrot, Benoit; Self-Organization; Snowflakes and Snow Crystals**

*Fractal patterns of tree branching (with eagles), 2019.*

# GEOMETER

A geometer is a specialist skilled in geometry or a practitioner of geometry. The origin of the term goes back to the Greek, with *geo* meaning "earth" or sometimes "global" and *metria* referring to a "measurer." Early tools of a geometer were the compass and ruler; today, electron microscopes and computers assist discoveries about geometry at all scales.

SEE ALSO: **Geometry; Two-Dimensional and Three-Dimensional Geometry**

# GEOMETRY

Geometry is the field of mathematics that deals with lines, points, shapes, and space. It is subdivided into different types such as two-dimensional and three-dimensional geometry as well as plane geometry (which deals with flat or two-dimensional shapes such as triangles, squares, and circles) and solid geometry (which deals with solid or three-dimensional shapes such as pyramids, cubes, and spheres).

SEE ALSO: **Circle and Sphere; Ellipse; Hexagon; Line; Mathematics; Platonic Solids; Rectangle and Parallelogram; Square and Cube; Triangle and Pyramid; Two-Dimensional and Three-Dimensional Geometry**

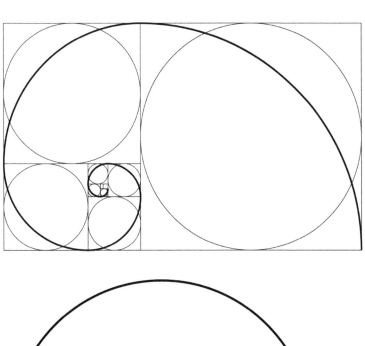

*The golden mean represented as a spiral in a golden rectangle and in a circle.*

# GOLDEN MEAN

*Greek letter for phi.*

The golden mean, also called the golden section, divine proportion, golden number, or golden ratio, refers to the ratio for length to width of rectangles. In mathematics, its numeric value is known as phi, the Greek letter φ.

Phi has a value of 1.618033988749895 . . . with the decimal occurring forever, although it is usually rounded off at 1.618. Universally, phi is considered to be sacred because it appears in many of nature's life-forms, such as the logarithmic spiral of the nautilus shell. When it's used in art and architecture, we typically see the work as beautiful and most pleasing to the eye.

Phi divides a line or rectangle into two unequal parts. The proportion of the two parts is the same as the proportion of the larger of the two parts to the original line. The ratio of the two then becomes 1:1.618 . . . Because the division can go on indefinitely, phi suggests never-ending replication and growth.

By using the ratio of 1.618 . . . as the sides of a rectangle, it becomes a golden rectangle. The golden mean also produces what are called the golden triangle and the golden pentagram, or five-pointed star.

Charles Hubbard, a biodynamic farmer in Nova Scotia, Canada, constructed his garden beds using this ratio; he saw an increase in plant growth and increased vitality in the food he produced.

SEE ALSO: **Numbers; Spiral**

# HELIX

The term *helix* comes from both Latin and Greek, meaning "spiral" or "spiral-shaped thing," and refers to the twisting shape of a corkscrew or a spiral staircase. In mathematics, it is a curve in three-dimensional space.

A double helix is a pair of parallel helices that are intertwined around a common axis. The three-dimensional structure of the double-stranded DNA molecule (the two DNA strands are oriented in different directions) is one of the most common examples of a double helix. DNA is called the "blueprint of life" because it holds the instructions by which an organism grows, develops, survives, and reproduces. The paired structure of the double helix provides stability and strength so that the DNA is not easily damaged or destroyed.

Mario Livio, an astronomer and theoretical astrophysicist, has identified a limited number of symmetries by which our universe is defined, one of which is known as screw symmetry. This is the type of symmetry of a corkscrew, where rotation about some axis is combined with translation along that axis. Some stems of plants also exhibit screw symmetry—the leaves appear at regular intervals after completing the same fraction of a full circle around the stem.[58]

Another is glide-reflection symmetry, exhibited by footprints generated by an alternating left-right-left-right walk. Glide-reflection symmetric designs create a snakelike visual sensation. Real snakes, which can form a circle and have bilateral movement, achieve these patterns by alternately contracting and relaxing muscle groups on both sides of their

*Screw symmetry is illustrated in this tree growing in a corkscrew shape in Mongolia. The explanation for its growth pattern is a metaphysical one—it is said to be growing on the intersection of energy lines. Buddhist monks smear it with butter, and viewers drape it with Buddhist prayer flags in recognition of its sacred nature.*

*Tribal painting from India showing intertwined snakes as a double helix.*

bodies—when they contract a group on the right, the corresponding group on the left is relaxed, and vice versa.[59]

The snake is an elemental form and recurring symbol of immortality in many cultures and is revered in many contexts as the origin of life. Anthropologist Jeremy Narby documents the parallels between the knowledge systems of molecular biology and Indigenous Peoples when he discusses the snake motif in terms of the double helix DNA. Noting the vast number of cultural traditions that speak of "cosmic serpents," he describes the snake as the origin or creator of life.[60]

SEE ALSO: **Fibonacci Sequence; Spiral; Symmetry**

# HEXAGON

A hexagon is a six-sided polygon, or what is called a 6-gon in geometry. The total of the internal angles of any simple hexagon is 720 degrees. The term comes from the Greek *hex* (meaning "six") and *gonía* (meaning "corner" or "angle").

Another way to look at a hexagon is that it is made up of six equilateral triangles.

In nature, honeycombs are hexagonal in shape. The cells start out as circles, then the circles flatten out under the pressure of being packed together. As they do so, they turn into hexagons to fill up the available space in the most efficient way.

SEE ALSO: **Beehives and Honeycombs; Polygon; Triangle and Pyramid**

# HEXAGRAM

A hexagram is a six-pointed star-like figure consisting of two equilateral triangles placed concentrically; each side of a triangle is parallel to a side of the other and on opposite sides of the center.[61] In I Ching, a hexagram is simply a figure of six stacked lines that are either solid or broken.

SEE ALSO: **Hexagon; I Ching**

*A hexagram composed of two overlapping triangles.*

# THE HIDDEN MESSAGES IN WATER

*The Hidden Messages in Water* is a book by Masaru Emoto, a Japanese author and scientist. Although his work and methods were heavily criticized, his book captured the imaginations of so many people that the book became a *New York Times* best seller. Emoto claimed, and illustrated using high-speed photography, that crystals formed in frozen water reveal changes when subjected to thoughts, sounds, and intentions. Benevolent, loving thoughts produce pleasing symmetrical patterns in the water, whereas fearful and negative thoughts result in discordance and disfigurement.

*Kali trampling Shiva. Chromolithograph by R. Varma. Date: before 1906.*

# HINDUISM

Hindu cosmology is based on the number four. Four yugas (epochs) characterize the existence of the universe from its origin or creation to its dissolution. However, since creation is cyclical and never-ending, each cycle consists of cosmic creation and destruction, with each age seeing the progressive decline of dharma, literally "that which upholds creation." Dharma usually refers to the harmony of the universe, a righteous code of conduct, sacred duty, or eternal law.[62]

In the first epoch, Satya Yuga, dharma or truth (satya) predominated. The second age is Treta Yuga, in which the universe lost one quarter of the truth. The third is Dvāpara Yuga, in which one half of the truth had been lost. The fourth is Kali Yuga, the one we live in now, where only one quarter of the truth remains, the remainder having been replaced by dishonesty and evil and a preoccupation with the physical body and materialism. Kali, meaning "The Dark One," is the destroyer of time (kala) and the destroyer of ego and is an aspect of the Divine Mother. She destroys the ego in order to transform and liberate humanity.[63] After the dissolution, the universe is recreated once again, and humankind becomes again truthful and righteous. It is only through destruction that final emancipation can come about.

In the Hindu pantheon, there exist 33 crore (330 million) deities, which may be interpreted as the one indivisible God-head taking on an infinite number of forms.

SEE ALSO: **Numbers**

# HOLOGRAPHIC UNIVERSE

A hologram is a three-dimensional image produced by the interference of light beams projecting from a laser or similar light source. The image retains the properties, such as depth and parallax, of the original object or scene. Every part of it contains the whole; thus, it can be taken apart and reduced to its smallest bit, which will retain the entire image.[64] As with a fractal, the whole is represented in every smaller piece. Holography is the science and practice of making holograms. The adjective *holographic* means "produced using holograms."

In opposition to a mechanistic, rational, and analytic view of the world that the West has embraced since Plato, a current question in the new sciences is whether we live in a sort of holographic universe, suggesting that reality as we know it is an illusion, that what we perceive as a tangible, physical, and three-dimensional universe may not be real after all.

In a holographic universe, nothing is separate from the whole, a view shared by such spiritual traditions as Buddhism and Hinduism. Such a holistic view of the universe appears in the ancient Buddhist Diamond Sutra: "In the house [meaning Heaven] of Indra there is said to be a network of pearls so arranged that if you look at one you see all the others reflected in it. In the same way, each object in the world is not merely itself but involves every other object, and in fact is every other object."[65]

It's also exhibited in this well-known quote from 13th-century Persian poet, Sufi mystic, and Islamic scholar Rumi: "You are an ocean in a drop of dew."[66]

One recent study suggests that holography offers a new framework for understanding the structure of the universe in line with the views of scientists such as 20th-century physicist David Bohm.[67] Bohm has been the main proponent of the holographic model of reality, proposing that every element of reality is related to everything else and that the whole is greater than the sum of its parts. In his view, reality is an "undivided wholeness,"[68] the universe is a kind of giant, flowing hologram, and "the tangible reality of our everyday lives is really a kind of illusion, like a holographic image."[69]

Although the idea is controversial, the holographic paradigm may even apply to the brain and to consciousness. In a holographic model of the brain, consciousness and reality are about relationship and process, reminding us that each of us exists as part of some larger whole. In such a model, the universe itself may possess a consciousness of which human consciousness is one expression.[70]

SEE ALSO: **Buddhism; Fractal; Geometry; Hinduism**

# I CHING

The I Ching, or "Book of Changes," is an ancient system of divination—an oracle—that has been in use in China for more than 3,000 years. Based in the dualism of Taoism, its

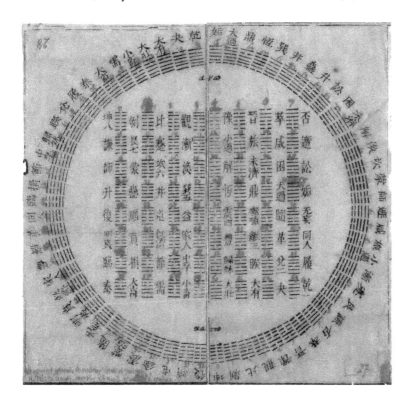

*A diagram of I Ching hexagrams sent to Gottfried Wilhelm Leibniz from Joachim Bouvet, a French Jesuit who worked in China. (The Arabic numerals were added by Leibniz.) Leibniz, who was corresponding with Jesuits in China, wrote the first European commentary on the I Ching in 1703.*

antagonistic and complementary principles of yin and yang endlessly rearrange themselves by both creating and destroying each other. The I Ching employs 64 hexagrams, which are all the possible ways to arrange six solid or broken lines that change back and forth between the dualistic yin and yang. The hexagram is a sort of characteristic combination of the two yin and yang lines engaged in endless change. The lines, arranged in groups of six, also represent all possible situations, institutions, and forms of change.

The I Ching has been related to early schools of Chinese astronomy and astrology, including what are called the 12 zodiacal places, and thus to universal and elemental patterns of the cosmos. It describes the multiple facets of the universe by means of a finite set of symbols. Seekers ask questions such as "Is it favorable for me to do x?" or "How many days will it take for me to accomplish x?"

In the West, Carl Jung used the I Ching with his patients in his psychotherapy practice, and Jungian psychology has been inspired by Taoist psychology.

SEE ALSO: **Hexagram; Zodiac**

# IAMBLICHUS
## (c. 250–c. 330)

The Syrian philosopher Iamblichus is credited with attempting to develop a theology that encompassed the rites, myths, and divinities of Paganism. This displaced the earlier spiritual and intellectual mysticism of the philosopher Plotinus in favor of theurgy, the magical conjuration of the gods: Whereas Plotinus viewed the One and the Good as the same, Iamblichus maintained the existence of a higher singularity or One beyond human knowledge and qualifications.[71] Theurgy is the operation or effect of a supernatural or divine agency in human affairs and included a system of white magic.[72] Because of Iamblichus's emphasis on the virtues by which ecstatic union is obtained with the One and his elevation of nonintellectual virtues, he was known for 200 years as "the divine" or "inspired."[73]

SEE ALSO: **Plotinus**

# INFINITY SYMBOL

Seventeenth-century English clergyman and mathematician John Wallis is credited with introducing the symbol that represents the concept of infinity. A mathematician and ordained priest, he was appointed professor of geometry at the University of Oxford. Derived from the Latin *infinitas*, or "unboundedness," the infinity symbol is a concept of mathematics and physics that refers to a quantity with no end or limitations.

In a spiritual sense, it has come to mean balance and harmony and the uniting of seemingly irreconcilable differences as well as the limitless and eternal nature of the Divine.

# INSECTS

*"If we were to wipe out insects alone on this planet, the rest of life and humanity with it would mostly disappear from the land. Within a few months."*[74]
—E. O. Wilson

Scientists and naturalists are discovering more and more about the geometric patterns by which insects organize themselves. This is called self-organization, or sometimes spontaneous order, referring, according to Roland Wedlich-Söldner and Timo Betz, "to the emergence of an overall order in time and space of a given system that results from the collective interactions of its individual components" and is core to pattern formation in chemistry, physics, and biology.[75]

British mathematician Alan Turing offered a mathematical model and the initial theory about how the markings of animal patterns, like a zebra's stripes or a ladybug's spots, are formed. His work has been applied to pattern formation in many areas—how fingers form, wave patterns, sand ripples on dunes, the patterns on butterfly wings or peacock feathers, the arrangement of leaves on a plant stem, how fish move in schools, and the arrangement of "ant cemeteries" where ants place their dead.

American biologist and naturalist E. O. Wilson has specialized in the study of ants. His 1971 book *The Insect Societies*, about ants and other insects, has become a classic. Among

*The polka dot patterns, also called "fairy circles," of the Namib Desert as seen from above.*

his many discoveries, Wilson uncovered how ants communicate—primarily through transmitting chemical substances called pheromones. He looked for mathematical models to explain the genetic evolution of culture. In studying ants and ant societies or colonies as superorganisms, he showed how each ant interacts with others so that the sum of the parts becomes greater than the whole. Self-organization seems to explain how much of biology "works"—from the interaction of molecules that produce animal markings to whole communities interacting to build their habitat. As an example, termites, using pheromones to communicate and incorporating self-organization, have created a vast 4,000-year-old pattern of mounds[76] spanning 230,000 kilometers in northeast Brazil. The mounds resulted from excavating interconnecting tunnel networks. Their work deposited soil in 200 million conical mounds that measure 2.5 meters in height each. The termites took advantage of episodic leaf fall to gather and store food in the tunnels and also maximized the removal of waste soil. Satellite images show a vast polka-dot pattern on the landscape. The mounds are distributed evenly—the termites have organized themselves into large colonies of equal size, which maximizes productivity since resources are not wasted or unused. But the pattern also minimizes aggression since one colony cannot take over another, as shown by the work of Corina Tarnita, another termite researcher.

Using mathematical ecology to model the impact of termites on plants in Kenya, Tarnita[77] shows how termites influence landscape on a large scale. They organize the landscape in a basic lattice of hexagons, foraging from their mounds in a widening circle. Over time, a single termite mound will bump up against another mound, at which point each builds up in size so they are equal, meaning one colony cannot take over another. Then they space themselves evenly across the landscape so that most mounds will have six neighbors in a self-organized hexagonal territory. Further, the regularity of the mounds across the landscape boosts the productivity of plants, resulting in taller grasses and bigger trees; plants associated with a termite mound are able to survive on less water than elsewhere. Simply put, termite mounds produce a more drought-resistant landscape.

It's astonishing to think that insects operate on principles of geometry that match and even supersede the complexities and scale of human engineering!

SEE ALSO: **Beehives and Honeycombs; Hexagon; Self-Organization**

# ISLAMIC ARTS AND ARCHITECTURE

Islamic architecture is known universally for its features such as the cupola, horseshoe arch, half-dome, and tunnel vault, and for its dazzlingly beautiful geometric tile patterns that repeat and interlace. Because Islam prohibits representations of the human form, complex geometric patterns replaced human representations in art and architecture, and mathematics was raised to an art in itself.

> *According to the Quran, "the work of God is unique and unrepeatable. Therefore, representations of animal and human figures are very rare because they are considered to be an attempt at imitating the work of God and competing with His genius. Representing God is unthinkable in Islam, and it is considered an offensive act of blasphemy . . . "[78]*
> —David Juliao, "Islamic Geometric Patterns: Religious Influences and Examples"

Four basic shapes—circles, squares, stars (made up of squares and triangles), and multisided polygons—are the most common in Islamic arts, but they can be combined into elaborate, complex, and seemingly endless patterns that suggest growth and expansion on the physical and metaphysical planes. Their awe-inspiring symmetry suggests balance and equanimity. Muslim artists actually discovered all the forms of symmetry that could be portrayed on a two-dimensional surface.

Along with geometric forms, designs based on motifs from nature, called arabesque, appear; the term refers to floral motifs that combine lines with flowers, tree branches, leaves, and so on. Even so, these are very stylized so that they do not appear to imitate God's creations.

SEE ALSO: **Circle and Sphere; Polygon; Square and Cube**

*Ceramic tile decorating a vault at the Nasir-ol-Molk Mosque in Shiraz, Iran.*

# JAPANESE GARDENS

Shinto was the traditional religion of Japan before Buddhism was introduced from China with its ideas of feng shui and yin/yang. The two traditions blended in Japan's gardens, which embody a reverence for nature and are designed as spiritual places that cultivate Zen ways of being. They remind us of our place in the universe and in the natural order of things and put us in touch with the power and grandeur of nature.

Where traditional Western gardens are based on symmetry, Japanese gardens incorporate asymmetry. Zen does not find harmony in designs based on pairs or on even numbers; instead, asymmetry is considered closer to nature and to the natural order. Thus, odd numbers of plants, rocks, and other elements will be grouped together to symbolize different ideas about life. Three, for example, represents the unity of humanity, earth, and heaven. Also auspicious are the numbers five and seven.

*"In everything, no matter what it may be, uniformity is undesirable. Leaving something incomplete makes it interesting, and gives one the feeling that there is room for growth."*[79]
—Yoshida Kenkō (c. 1283–c. 1350/52)

Classical Zen gardens were designed by Japanese monks as places of meditation and contemplation, to provide feelings of equilibrium, tranquility, and ultimately peace, and where the spirit is nurtured to grow on its path through comprehension of life's true meaning. As the Buddha achieved enlightenment (under a tree), so may concentration, perseverance, and staying on one's spiritual path lead one to enlightenment. Such gardens create feelings of space and expansiveness even in tiny, limited spaces, suggesting a world larger than the area occupied. The designs put one directly in touch with nature but also allow for the viewer's own imagination and senses to interpret the garden and its symbolism.

Rocks, water, sand, plants—each element is given form to convey particular ideas about spirituality. Rocks show time in its greatest scope and therefore may be used to symbolize the impermanence of life or to illustrate the ravages of time. Water is revered as vital to life and may symbolize all the facets of water from calm to turbulent. The Buddhist aspiration of "no mind," or a mind empty of thought, may be symbolized by sand. Rocks on sand may represent how our thoughts should be "balanced," and rocks will be placed in groups so that each group is balanced in itself and also in relation to the whole. Misshapen trees that have withstood the storms of life symbolize triumph over adversity, whereas evergreen conifers may be used to symbolize longevity. A plant such as the camellia may represent death in the midst of life because its beautiful flowers tend to fall in mid-bloom.

> *"I like to wash,*
> *the dust of this world*
> *In the droplets of dew."*[80]
> —Matsuo Basho (1644–1694)

SEE ALSO: **Feng Shui; Symmetry**

# JENNY, HANS

## SEE CYMATICS (p. 27)

# KEPLER, JOHANNES

## (1571–1630)

Johannes Kepler was a German mathematician, astrologer, and astronomer who is well known for his application of sacred geometry to astronomy. His many discoveries included charting that the paths of planets are ellipses. His work also marked the transition from the earth-centered view of the universe of his time to the heliocentric, sun-centered view that we hold today. He revived the ancient idea of the harmony of the spheres, associating musical notes with the orbits of planets.

SEE ALSO: **Ellipse; Music of the Spheres**

# LEY LINES

The early mapping and naming of ley lines are attributed to Alfred Watkins. He noticed that across the British countryside, features such as burial mounds, beacon hills, churches, crossroads, holy wells, and old stone crosses were connected by straight lines that he interpreted as the remains of ancient tracks or trading routes. The second of his two books, *The Old Straight Track* (1925),[81] remains in print and has fueled innumerable theories about their purpose all over the world, although his ideas have not been accepted by archaeology or mainstream science. Watkins, however, did not attribute mystical or energetic properties to the lines. Instead, he proposed that the early pre-Roman inhabitants of Britain were aware that the shortest distance between two points was a straight line and thus set up paths that allowed them to move around the country in the most efficient way. Along these routes they lined up markers—hills, boulders, clumps of trees, ponds—which would be visible for miles. Although these original trackways became lost over time, markers remained to become markets and meeting places, burial sites, pagan temples, and other places of significance for the peoples that followed. Eventually, such sites would become obvious locations for Christian churches.

At a 2004 Moscow conference on shamanism in Siberia,[82] researchers spoke about equivalent lines to Watkins' ley lines, called dragon's lines or dragon's sinew in China and spirit roads in North America, but these ideas have not been authenticated in the scholarly literature. In 2009, at Scotland's Rosslyn Chapel, made famous in Dan Brown's *The Da Vinci*

*Code*, a guide pointed out a keystone that, she suggested, may point to where two ley lines cross in the chapel; one of these lines she called a Rose Line, which, she noted, connects chapels and other sacred sites around the world.[83]

Purev Otgony, writing on Mongolian shamanism, cites studies in the Lake Hovsgol area of what are called water spirits in English. Each one of these "has a direct path between two tangible points that remains constant" so that people can avoid crossing its path and avoid misfortune.[84] The distance between the two end points ranges from a few meters to many kilometers. Perhaps these are ley lines in another cultural context.

SEE ALSO: **Line; Shamanism**

# LINE

Euclid defined a line as an interval between two points that could be extended indefinitely in either direction. In mathematical terms, a line is one-dimensional.

SEE ALSO: **Dimension; Euclid**

# LOTUS

A sacred flower in Eastern religions such as Buddhism and Hinduism, the lotus represents the mind's transcendent nature. It is a symbol of the purity of the Bodhisattva, a person on the path to Buddhahood and the final goal of Nirvana, who delays attainment out of compassion in order to save suffering beings. Divine figures are often shown seated on a lotus flower; it is the pedestal of Lord Buddha.

The lotus grows in muddy water, its roots bound in earthly attachment, while its flower opens to the light of the heavens. It may be represented in different stages from the fully open flower to the half-open flower, and its different colors—white, blue, pink—have different associations.

> *"One who performs his duty without attachment, surrendering the results unto the Supreme Lord, is unaffected by sinful action, as the lotus is untouched by water."*
> —From *The Bhagavad Gita,* Chapter 5, Text 10, the ancient Indian text important to Hinduism (meaning *The Song of the Lord*)

SEE ALSO: **Buddhism; Hinduism**

# MANDALA

Mandalas, like medicine wheels, incorporate elemental and universal geometrical forms such as the circle, square, and equidistant cross. They manifest the unseen world of the sacred, bringing together the sacred and the mundane, the physical and metaphysical, thus providing a sort of template by which we may live in alignment with these universal principles.

A mandala is basically a geometric structure composed of a square within a circle. The circle usually represents the Divine, eternity, or the all-pervading consciousness; the square generally represents this physical plane. These two elemental forms are then combined with other geometric shapes such as the triangle and equidistant, four-sided cross. In Buddhist and Hindu symbolism, in the Shamanic/Buddhist Bön tradition of Tibet, and in Tantra, a mandala represents the wholeness of the universe or perhaps the search for wholeness in an individual. A mandala is also a visual representation of sacred sounds or mantras and an expression of cosmic vibratory patterns that give form and structure to the physical, material world.

The word *mandala* derives from the Sanskrit meaning "disk," but the term is now widely used cross-culturally to describe what has become a more or less universal form or combination of forms. The basic mandala form, as well as its component elements, is found in many spiritual traditions and in many time periods, such as the prehistoric rock art of the Americas. Science suggests that such elemental forms and patterns are due to the architecture of the human brain's neural network.[85] Mandalas thus become a manifestation of the human mind.

*Mandala of the 19th-century Tibetan school.*

SEE ALSO: **Circle and Sphere; Mantra; Medicine Wheel; Numbers; Sacred Geometry; Square and Cube; Yantra**

# MANDELBROT, BENOIT

## (1924–2010)

Benoit Mandelbrot, called the "father of fractal geometry," developed an entire new branch of mathematics and geometry called fractals. Fractals have been called the geometry of nature and are still being explored in mathematics and science. Mandelbrot discovered that he could plot millions and even billions of points by programming a computer instead of doing so manually. Simply put, he began with a particular expression in algebra and then substituted a complex number into that expression. He then programmed his computer to generate the answer, plot it, and plug it back into the equation. He was able to keep going into the billions of points because the computer could handle the size of the resulting graph. He discovered that small regions of the set looked like smaller-scale copies of the entire set,[86] and thus came the idea of fractals.

SEE ALSO: **Fractal**

# MANTRA

A mantra is a constantly repeated sacred formula or prayer. It awakens the dormant spiritual powers within to help us reach the goal of spiritual awakening. Mantras are especially potent when they are received from a spiritual master.[87] Mantric power or spiritual energy is concentrated in the letters of the

The sacred sound OM, sometimes written as Aum, inscribed here in Sanskrit. Related to the religions of Buddhism, Hinduism, and Jainism, it has now become a widespread symbol of New Age spirituality.

mantra. Reciting a mantra activates the vitalizing force within a seeker who is reciting not words or elements of grammar but symbols that express what cannot be described in language in terms of resonating wavicles of sound vibrations. (Wavicles are entities with properties of both waves and particles.) Simple mantras are composed of "atomic" monosyllabic sounds such as Hrīm or Krīm, whereas more complex ones incorporate sequences of these basic sounds. The basic sounds are called seed mantras, each of which contains the quintessential powers of divinity.[88] The sacred sound OM is the best-known seed mantra and, as the primordial sound, is associated with the universe in all of its manifestations.

> "Our mind pulls us in all directions. Through the mantra, one tries to focus the mind, and through that we gain energy. As a magnifying glass converges the rays of the sun to a point of such an intensity that it can produce fire, so, through spiritual practices, one can gather much energy to do good for the world. If a normal person can be compared to a light bulb, a tapasvi (a serious practitioner) is like a transformer."[89]
> —Mata Amritanandamayi Math, "MA OM Meditation and Mantra Japa"

Different mantras serve different purposes, from inducing trance to enhancing meditation to invoking protection from negative forces. And the subtle vibrations of mantras intensify the power of the yantra with which they are associated.

SEE ALSO: **Buddhism; Hinduism; Yantra**

# MATHEMATICS

Mathematics, in the view of author Steven Scott Pither, is not actually composed of numbers and the principles that express relationships between numbers. Instead, mathematics is about *ideas*—the idea of numbers and the idea of relationship. The system of mathematics, he points out, is a mental concept. Mathematics has no actual physical existence in and of itself, but it does have a structure and a form, albeit an elastic, elusive, and ethereal kind of form. And so it can be applied, in Pither's view, to anything that has form: "Mathematics is capable of representing, or modelling, the inner and outer natures of anything."[90] That can include the spiritual path. Thus, metaphysical concepts and constructs may be expressed mathematically. In this way, the universal language of mathematics is a key to the mysteries of the universe.

There have been many mathematical systems throughout the world, from that of the Romans who could count from one to ten thousand using their fingers to that of a tribe of South Sea Islanders for whom two is the highest number; they count from one to five in the following manner:

$$1, 2, 2'1, 2'2, 2'2'1[91]$$

Today, we use a mathematical system with what's called a base of 10, whereby each numeral's position (1–9 and 0) is based off the power of 10. Bases of other than 10 have been used by such cultures as the Chinese, Maya, Aztecs, Druids, and Sumerians. For the latter, which used a base of 60, nature was the source of what they considered to be sacred numbers—the length of the year, objects seen in the skies, and so on; the stars, moon, and sun were believed to be divine beings and the cycles of the orbits were the gods in action.[92]

For most of us, the spiritual or sacred source of our numbering system has been obscured, but we can go back to its roots to understand and reconnect with its cultural and metaphysical aspects. Doing so ultimately alters our views of reality.

Many difficult mathematical problems remain unsolved. Mathematics may be a pure science and sacred geometry the hidden code of the universe, but so many mysteries remain that are incomprehensible to the layperson and even as yet unattainable to the most accomplished mathematician. Author Keith Devlin explains it this way: Although a century ago a mathematical problem could be explained to the interested layperson, the level of abstraction required to understand mathematics has increased over time. This is because the human brain must work hard to achieve a new level of abstraction: "Only when one new level has been mastered is it possible to abstract from that level to yet another level. This is part of the reason why it takes so many years for a young mathematician to reach the frontiers of certain branches of the subject."[93] Perhaps mathematics itself is evolving the human brain so that it is more and more capable of comprehending the mysteries of the sacred structure of the universe.

SEE ALSO: **Geometry; Numbers; Pythagoras**

# MEDICINE WHEEL

Medicine wheels, like mandalas, incorporate elemental and universal geometrical forms such as the circle and the equidistant cross. They manifest the sacred geometry of the unseen world, providing a sort of template by which we may live in alignment with universal principles.

Among First Nations and Métis of Canada and Native Americans of the United States, the medicine wheel— sometimes called the circle of life or sacred hoop—may be viewed as an equivalent form to the Hindu and Buddhist mandala. Divided into equivalent fourths, it portrays the overall circle of life and, within it, transitions such as the four seasons, the four life stages, the four elements, and so on. Medicine wheels laid out in the landscape may be huge and used ceremonially by large groups of people. They may be solar and lunar calendars or constellation effigies or serve some other purpose. Or they may be small-scale individual charts of one's life journey for healing and spiritual purposes. The massive Bighorn Medicine Wheel in Wyoming measures 80 feet in diameter. Stones are laid out in a wheel-like pattern with 28 spoke-like lines emanating from the center. Built by

*Bighorn Medicine Wheel
in Wyoming.*

Plains Indians about 300 to 800 years ago, it has since been maintained and used by various Native American groups for ceremony.

Archaeologist Gordon Freeman, however, suggests that the term has outlived its usefulness because it has been applied too generally. Instead, he suggests different purposes to structures that have been grouped together as medicine wheels.[94]

Science suggests that such elemental forms and patterns are due to the architecture of the human brain's neural network.[95] Thus, medicine wheels become a manifestation of the human mind and, in a sacred sense, of the mind of the Creator.

SEE ALSO: **Circle and Sphere; Mandala; Mantra; Numbers; Sacred Geometry; Square and Cube**

# MÖBIUS BAND

The Möbius band or strip was discovered by and named after August Ferdinand Möbius, an 18th-century German mathematician and theoretical astronomer best known for its discovery. He answered a mathematical conundrum: Does a two-dimensional surface have one or two sides? Though "two" would seem the obvious answer, the Möbius band shows that it is possible to construct a surface with only one side when it is embedded in a three-dimensional space. Though made from a two-sided piece of paper, the Möbius strip has only one side and only one edge.

You can demonstrate his finding. Start by taking a long, thin piece of paper about a foot long and an inch wide. (The paper will have two sides to start.) Make a half twist in the paper, then paste together the two ends to form a twisted band. You'll discover that the band is one-sided. With a pencil, pick a point in the middle of the loop and draw a line around the loop down the middle of the band—the pencil line goes around the loop twice and comes back to the starting point.

A Möbius band also has only one edge. Using a colored pencil, color the edge of the band. The entire edge will become colored as a single unit—there will be no uncolored edge. Also, by drawing a small left hand on the surface of the strip and then making adjacent copies until you get back to where you started, you'll discover that the left hand has become a right hand.[96] The Möbius band is a good illustration of the many mysteries and unexplained puzzles that remain in mathematics.

SEE ALSO: **Mathematics**

# MOLECULAR GEOMETRY

The term *molecular geometry* refers to the three-dimensional arrangement of the atoms that make up a molecule. Water and oxygen are examples of molecules that are particles made up of at least two chemically bonded atoms. The geometry of the molecule determines each atom's position.

SEE ALSO: **Atom; Geometry**

# MOLECULE

In biology and chemistry, the term *molecule* refers to a very small piece of something—a tiny particle or substance, especially at the structural or cellular level. Made up of two or more atoms held together by a strong chemical bond, a molecule is the smallest unit of an element or compound.[97] Albert Einstein is credited with confirming the existence of atoms and molecules and also with the calculations that made it possible to determine their otherwise invisible size.

> *"Look deep into nature, and then you will understand everything better."*[98]
> —Albert Einstein

SEE ALSO: **Atom; Molecular Geometry; Theory of Relativity**

# MUSIC

Numbers and geometry codify the hidden order of creation; many scientists and artists, including Euclid, Pythagoras, and Plato, consider mathematics to be sacred. As mathematics is patterns, so music is patterns—rhythm, melody, time signatures, overtones, tones, intervals, harmonies, and scales made in sound. The universality and concrete application of numbers and geometry are embodied in music in all traditions. In fact, all music is mathematics at some level. The 19th-century English mathematician James Joseph Sylvester described the relationship between music and mathematics this way: "May not music be described as the mathematics of sense, mathematics as the music of reason, the soul of each the same?"[99]

Sounds or notes may be harmonious or discordant. Pythagoras discovered that whole numbers, such as one, two, three, four, and so on, govern musical harmonies and produce harmonious sounds, whether these exist at the macro level of the planetary orbits or the micro level of the strings of a guitar and how they're tuned. Only whole number ratios such as 1:2 and 3:5 produce harmonies. Ratios made up of other than whole numbers such as 3.7:4.5 produce dissonance. Whole number ratios are the basis of scales, and the ratios remain constant regardless of the key or the number of notes in a scale (which vary across cultures). Different scales and different keys produce different emotions; musicians explore the revelations that emerge when mathematical patterns are discovered and then transformed into music. Sometimes a composer will embed such patterns in their compositions to be discovered by the musician or the audience. In discussing the music of Johann Sebastian Bach, mathematician Mario Livio points out mathematical patterns on many levels, but particularly in Bach's canons: "Canons in general were considered at the time to be some sort of symmetry puzzles. The composer provided the theme, but it was the musicians' task to figure out what type of symmetry operation he had in mind for the theme to be performed . . . this is not very different conceptually from the puzzle posed to us by the universe—it lies in all its glory open to inspection—for us to find the underlying patterns and symmetries."[100]

SEE ALSO: **Euclid; Mathematics; Numbers; Pythagoras; Plato; Symmetry**

*From* Theorica musicae *by Franchino Gaffurio, woodcut showing Pythagoras with bells, a kind of glass harmonica, a monochord, and pipes in Pythagorean tuning. The bells, glasses, hammers, flutes, and strings are calibrated 4, 6, 8, 9, 12, 16—all whole numbers.*

# MUSIC OF THE SPHERES

That there is a music of the spheres or planets is an ancient idea. Pythagoras, for example, is known for the statement "There is geometry in the humming of the strings, there is music in the spacing of the spheres."[101] In ancient times, it was generally believed that the song of each planet was based on the speed of its orbit because the vibrations caused by its motion through space would create sound waves. People believed the planets moved in circular paths at constant speeds, that each planet consequently sang one note, and that such music was therefore one never-ending chord.[102]

Then came Johannes Kepler, the 17th-century German astrologer, astronomer, and mathematician, who played a key role in the scientific revolution. He is best known for his discovery of the laws of planetary motion and a hypothetical music based on them. His discovery that planets move in elliptical paths and at different speeds changed the concept of the celestial chord. Instead, Kepler calculated the changing speeds of each planet and converted those speeds into tones, theorizing that the music of the spheres was a continuous and ever-changing song.

Kepler, however, created the music in theory and never actually heard it because there was no technology available to capture or produce such sounds. With the help of computer scientists and a synthesizer, Willie Ruff, an associate professor of music at Yale University, and John Rodgers, a pianist and Silliman Professor of Geology at Yale, synthesized the music of the spheres based on Kepler's calculations, notations, and theories, making Kepler's music audible 350 years later.[103]

Harmony of the World, *a heliocentric universe showing the planets' correct distances and the zodiacal signs, with Aries beginning at the horizon and the other signs following in correct order, dated 1806.*

SEE ALSO: **Kepler, Johannes; Music; Pythagoras**

# NETWORKS

Recent scientific discoveries reveal how an underlying architecture with shared organizing principles governs various complex systems. Such revelations have become part of an emerging field of mathematics focusing on what are called random networks. Although random, these networks still behave in certain predictable ways that can be measured mathematically.[104]

An obvious example of a network is the brain, a network of nerve cells that are composed of networks of molecules. Other examples include species, languages, computer systems, biology, transportation systems, and entire societies. But how can such seemingly different systems obey the same laws and have the same architecture? The authors of such a study on scale-free networks, Albert-László Barabási and Eric Bonabeau, propose a mathematical formula to describe the property that particular networks share but point out that the reasons underlying it are "not yet known."[105]

Such studies point out how mathematics is an evolving disciple with many—perhaps limitless—mysteries to be revealed. They also enhance our understanding of the complex, interconnected worlds in which we live, both human-made and nature-based.

SEE ALSO: **Cell Structure and Function; Mathematics; Molecule**

# NUMBERS

Numbers are mental constructs with no actual physical presence in and of themselves. They are "known" but are "unseen" and of the metaphysical, in the same way that the spirit world is unseen and not of this physical world. Thus, numbers may be said to be numinous or to have numinous qualities. From where do they originate, and what is their ultimate purpose? Mathematicians, philosophers, and metaphysicians remain fascinated with numbers without having all the answers to these and other questions.

## Prime and Composite Numbers

Mathematics has identified two types of numbers: prime and composite.

Prime numbers are a sort of cosmic mystery! They seem to have no order in their sequence and appear haphazardly among the composites. Yet they are very important in daily life, for example, for computer coding in banks and on the Internet; encryption systems based on primes are very difficult to break. A prime number is a positive integer. Integers are either positive or negative. Positive integers are numbers used in everyday counting: When you buy a dozen oranges, for example, you are using a positive integer. Primes are whole numbers, meaning numbers without decimals or fractions. A prime number has no divisors that are positive integers other than one and itself. The number 13 is a prime number because it can only be divided by 1 and 13; other primes include 2, 3, 5, 7, 11, and 17. As such, primes are the building blocks of all other numbers. Mathematicians have long been intrigued with prime numbers, trying to break their hidden code and puzzling over still-unanswered questions such as "Is there a definite pattern to their sequencing?"

Composite numbers, on the other hand, are positive integers that are not prime, such as the number 24, which is divisible by many numbers: 1, 2, 3, 4, 6, 8, and 12.

## The Number One

The number one is neither prime nor composite, which makes it interesting in terms of the sacred. The number one is indivisible and is also the base of other numbers. Thus, one in spiritual traditions often, if not always, represents God, the Divine, the Great Spirit, the Source, the Creator, the Un-nameable One, and so on, from which the multitude of expressions or "the many" manifest. The number one signifies the unity, the "oneness" of all of creation and the interconnectedness of all life. The Lakota Sioux are credited with the phrase "all my relations," which has become a common phrase used widely by Indigenous Peoples in North America and elsewhere as an illustration of the indivisible oneness of all of creation.

## The Number Two

The number two signifies the duality of existence, as in, for example, good/evil, seen world/unseen world, heaven/earth, and positive/negative. Some Native American cultures represent the duality as Father Sky/Mother Earth,

*Yin/yang is a concept of dualism from ancient Chinese philosophy.*

the sacred union of the cosmos. In such views, a balance of opposites must be maintained in order for the universe to operate properly.

Ancient Chinese philosophy represents the duality of existence as yin and yang, incorporating these opposing-yet-united forces into the encircled yin (female, weak, dark) and yang (male, strong, light). Such opposites are attracted to one another, and each needs the other to define itself.

## The Number Three

In shamanic traditions, the number three signifies the tripartite universe composed of the Upper, Middle, and Lower worlds; a shaman navigates the three worlds to provide healing, counseling, and direction in this, the Middle world, and to keep the worlds connected and operating harmoniously. In Christianity, the Father, Son, and Holy Ghost are the Holy Trinity.

## The Number Four

*The Holy Trinity by Miguel Cabrera (1695–1768).*

The number four is represented in the equidistant cross in which two equal pairs intersect, as in the Tibetan Bön mandalas or the medicine wheel of the Americas. Mandalas and medicine wheels may symbolize the four seasons (spring, summer, autumn, winter); the four directions (north, east, south, west); the four life stages (birth, childhood or infancy through adolescence, maturity or adulthood, and old age or death); and so on.

Different spiritual traditions build on these numbers and their combinations to express beliefs and practices.

SEE ALSO: **Mandala; Mathematics; Medicine Wheel; Pythagoras; Shamanism; Tripartite Universe**

# NUMEROLOGY

Numerology, or "number symbolism," explores the symbolic and spiritual meaning of numbers along with the mathematical processes of subtraction, addition, division, and multiplication. Defined by Steven Scott Pither as "part of an ancient system for understanding oneself and other people, for divination, and even for spirituality,"[106] numerology has had many variants such as the Kabalistic tree of life; the I Ching or Chinese Book of Changes, said to be a mathematical model of the universe; and Pythagorean numerology, the modern variant that developed in the 20th century. Numerology has changed over time, engendering contradictions and disagreements about its possibilities and applications. Many dismiss it as pseudoscience. Practitioners call it a science of numbers and see the possibility of bridging science and mysticism through its study to reveal a new model of reality that is both scientific and metaphysical.

SEE ALSO: **I Ching; Mathematics; Numbers; Pythagoras; Tree of Life**

# PARABOLA

A parabola is an open curve produced by the intersection of a right circular cone and a plane that is parallel to the side of the cone. A parabola is also symmetric about its axis. Certain bridges exhibit a parabolic shape, forming arches,[107] as do cathedrals, gates, roofs, and other architectural structures in many traditions. The suspension cables on the Golden Gate Bridge in San Francisco are parabolas. The traditional design of the Central Asian yurt incorporates a parabola shape.[108] Water shooting out from a fountain may be parabolic, as occurs with the spectacular Bellagio fountains in Las Vegas.

In a technical sense, a parabola is a mathematical expression of a particular geometric variation of the two-dimensional circle. A parabola retains the structural simplicity of a circle but in three-dimensional form. Simply put, a parabola is a circle that has been warped. Thus, it is an elemental form in the same way that a circle or a square is iconic.

Twentieth-century artist David Crockett Johnson produced artwork based on mathematics and mathematical physics, including illustrating a discussion of Archimedes' discoveries.[109]

SEE ALSO: **Archimedes; Circle and Sphere; Two-Dimensional and Three-Dimensional Geometry; Yurt**

*Fountains of Bellagio Hotel and Casino in Las Vegas, Nevada.*

# PI

Represented by the symbol π, the term *pi* refers to the ratio of the circumference of a circle to its diameter. Pi has a value of 3.141592653589793 ... with the decimal occurring forever, although it is usually rounded off at 3.14. Mathematicians from ancient times have grappled with the mystery of pi and how to represent the ratio, going as far back as 2000 BCE when the Babylonians used 3.125 to represent it. The ancient Egyptians and, later, Indian, Chinese, Arab, and European mathematicians extended the number of decimal points. It wasn't until recently, however, that computers allowed for pi to be calculated to more than 200,000,000,000 decimal places. But in everyday calculations, an approximation such as 22/7 is commonly used to represent the ratio.[110]

SEE ALSO: **Circle and Sphere**

# PLANTS

Plants, and especially their flowers, have captured our imaginations throughout the ages. Scientists and naturalists continue to be fascinated by their structure and function. Studies expand our knowledge almost daily, investigating, for example, how plants transport vital fluids in the most efficient way for the space they occupy. Artists and poets, on the other hand, challenge themselves to portray the ineffable beauty of a rose or a daffodil. And yet both approaches seem inextricably linked.

Leonardo da Vinci saw both beauty and function in his studies of the natural world and, specifically, in the precise geometric arrangement of leaves on a stem.

> *"The leaf always turns its upper side towards the sky so that it may be better able to receive the dew over its whole surface; and these leaves are arranged on the plants in such a way that one covers another as little as possible. This alternation provides open spaces through which the sun and air may penetrate. The arrangement is such that drops from the first leaf fall on the fourth leaf in some cases and on the sixth in others."[111]*
> —Leonardo Da Vinci

Plants exhibit all the properties of sacred geometry discussed in this book: the spiral of cactus spines, pinecones, and unfurled fern fronds; the fractal pattern of a tree's branches and roots; or the symmetry of leaf arrangements on the stem of a climbing pea plant. The pattern of leaves and the number of petals on most plants involve the Fibonacci numbers, while the golden mean organizes the seed arrangements of a sunflower. A stoma on the underside of a leaf forms an almond-shaped opening (the mathematically magical vesica piscis) as pairs of guard cells open and close to allow for gas exchange.

Like insects such as ants, plants, too, self-organize. They support and assist one another; in a sunny area, for example, being under the shade of a tree or bush can be beneficial for a tiny plant. They also compete for water and nutrients. Such interactions lead to the plants creating geometric patterns on the landscape—such as the repeated green/arid pattern—which both maximize accessibility to and distribute resources in the most efficient way possible.

We may have no sense of the geometry embedded in plants, but most of us respond intuitively to a beautiful flower. Just as our knowledge of the cosmos is expanding through mathematics, so we enter deeper into the mystery of even the simplest of nature's creations, thus learning about creation itself.

SEE ALSO: **da Vinci, Leonardo; Fractal; Golden Mean; Self-Organization; Spiral; Symmetry; Vesica Piscis**

# PLATO
## (c. 428/427–c. 348/347 BCE)

Plato viewed a core mathematical knowledge as key to developing an understanding of the universe. This core was to become known as the quadrivium. He outlined the curriculum in his *Republic*, which was written around 375 BCE. In it, he wrote: "Then, my noble friend, geometry will draw the soul towards truth, and create the spirit of philosophy, and raise up that which is not unhappily allowed to fall down."[112] He also wrote, "The Knowledge of which geometry aims is the knowledge of the eternal,"[113] thus capturing the essence of the meaning of sacred geometry. It is said that an inscription over the entrance to Plato's Academy in Athens read, "Let none but geometers enter here."[114]

In his *Timaeus*, which dates to about 360 BCE, cosmology and geometry are intertwined. He viewed perfected three-dimensional shapes such as cubes and pyramids as the "Platonic solids" out of which the whole universe is made. Underlying his account of the universe's formation and his explanation of its extraordinary order and beauty is the idea that the universe is the product of a rational, purposive, and beneficent agency, a divine "craftsman" who imposes mathematical order on preexisting chaos to generate the ordered universe.

SEE ALSO: Geometry; Mathematics; Platonic Solids; Quadrivium

# PLATONIC SOLIDS

The Platonic solids are the five geometric solids (three-dimensional figures), also called the five regular polyhedra, whose faces are all identical, regular polygons that meet at the same three-dimensional angle. The five are the tetrahedron or pyramid, the cube, the octahedron of eight plane faces, the dodecahedron of 12 faces, and the icosahedron of 20 faces. They are considered to be especially beautiful, as they are structurally symmetrical, thus they often appear in art and architecture. Over time, mathematicians such as Pythagoras, Euclid, and Plato discovered their various forms. Plato named them as an entire group and associated them with the four basic elements—fire (tetrahedron), earth (cube), air (octahedron), and water (icosahedron). In Plato's view, it was from

The five Platonic solids: octahedron, tetrahedron, cube, icosahedron, and dodecahedron.

the combinations of these four essentials that all matter took shape.[115] He then assigned the dodecahedron to the heavens because of its 12 constellations. Plato's theory of the universe led to the five becoming known as the Platonic solids. Centuries later, Johannes Kepler used the Platonic solids to explain the geometry of the universe in his model of the cosmos.[116]

In many spiritual traditions, the square or the four-square regularity of the cube also represents earth. In a mandala, for example, the square representing the earth is encased within a circle representing the heavens, the One, or the metaphysical realm.

SEE ALSO: **Euclid; Kepler, Johannes; Mandala; Plato; Polygon; Pythagoras**

## PLOTINUS (c. 204/5–c. 270)

Plotinus, an Egyptian-born philosopher, is generally regarded as one of the most influential philosophers of antiquity after Aristotle and Plato. In the essence of his writings on physics, cosmology, psychology, and metaphysics was the presence of an infinite and good supreme divinity. Plotinus claimed complete union with God, the One who is beyond all categories, without division and multiplicity, but is the source of all creation in its multiple forms. True happiness, in his view, could not be found in the material world, only in the metaphysical. Geometry, he wrote, "leads the human soul upwards to philosophical truth."[117] He also said, "You can only apprehend the Infinite by a faculty that is superior to reason."[118]

SEE ALSO: **Aristotle; Plato**

# POLYGON

A polygon is an enclosed flat figure made up of straight lines. The term comes from Greek via Latin meaning "many-angled." Many types of polygons exist; each is named for the number of sides it has. Here are some of the most common ones from three to ten:

**THREE SIDES:**
TRIANGLE

**FOUR SIDES:**
QUADRILATERAL
(Such as a square, rectangle, or parallelogram)

**FIVE SIDES:**
PENTAGON

**SIX SIDES:**
HEXAGON

**SEVEN SIDES:**
HEPTAGON

**EIGHT SIDES:**
OCTAGON

**NINE SIDES:**
NONAGON

**TEN SIDES:**
DECAGON

When the number of sides of a polygon gets really high, mathematicians might use $n$ and call it an $n$-gon; for example, if a polygon has 31 sides, it would be called a 31-gon.

SEE ALSO: **Hexagon; Rectangle and Parallelogram; Square and Cube; Triangle and Pyramid**

# PYTHAGORAS
## (c. 570–c. 490 BCE)

Pythagoreanism originated in the 6th century BCE, based on the teachings and beliefs of the Greek philosopher Pythagoras and his followers, the Pythagoreans. In their search for eternal universal laws, the Pythagoreans sought unchanging elements that underlay both human society and nature. According to some scholars, the quadrivium originated with Pythagoras around 500 BC; it became their organizing scheme.[119]

Pythagoras believed that the cosmos was structured according to moral principles and significant numerical relationships. He proposed that the heavenly bodies appeared to move in accordance with the mathematical ratios that govern the concordant musical intervals. Thus, they produced a music of the heavens, which later developed into what is commonly called the harmony of the spheres.[120]

Pythagoreans believed that numbers were magic, that "all is number" and "God is number." They practiced a kind of numerology or number-worship, with each number having its own character and meaning: One, for example, generated all numbers; two represented opinion; three represented harmony; four, justice; five, marriage; six, creation; seven, the seven planets or "wandering stars"; and so on. Odd numbers were thought of as female and even numbers as male. The holiest number was tetractys.[121]

SEE ALSO: **Music; Music of the Spheres; Numbers; Numerology; Quadrivium**

*Pythagoras the mathematician in* The School of Athens, *by the artist Raphael, from 1509.*

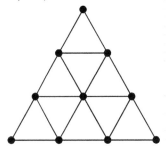

*The Pythagorean "tetractys" or "ten" as an equilateral triangle arranged as 10 points in four rows of one, two, three, and four. It was both a mathematical concept and a metaphysical symbol.*

# QUADRIVIUM

God as Architect/Builder/Geometer/ Craftsman, The Frontpiece of Bible Moralisee *by an anonymous artist from a 13th-century manuscript (c. 1220–1230). The compass symbolizes God's creation of the universe in adherence to geometric and harmonic principles. This illustration was famously used as the first color illustration in Benoit Mandelbrot's* The Fractal Geometry of Nature.

Seven liberal arts subjects formed the basis of the monastic system of education in medieval times. These were composed of the trivium and the quadrivium. The preparatory three verbal arts of the trivium were the foundation for the four mathematical arts of the quadrivium: arithmetic or numbers as abstract concepts, geometry, astronomy, and music. Arithmetic is concerned with the infinite linear array of numbers. Geometry moves beyond the line to higher-dimensional spaces. Music or harmony basically applies the pure science of numbers evolving in time. Astronomy applies geometry to the world of space.[122]

The term *quadrivium* comes from Latin, meaning "four ways"; its use for the four subjects has been attributed to both Roman philosopher Boethius and Roman scholar and statesman Cassiodorus, both active in the 6th century. Other scientists suggest that it originated even earlier, with Pythagoras, around 500 BCE.[123] The quadrivium then became the foundation for the study of philosophy and theology. Medieval scholarship was based in the belief that the universe was created by God according to specific geometric and harmonic principles. Thus, the fundamentals of the quadrivium were a direct link to the Divine; to seek knowledge of them was to seek God.

SEE ALSO: **Fractal; Mandelbrot, Benoit; Music; Pythagoras; Trivium**

# RAINBOW

A rainbow forms as sunlight is sprinkled about by raindrops that are close to spherical in shape. In 1637, René Descartes worked out the location of a rainbow relative to the sun and the observer. A few decades later, Isaac Newton explained the colors of a rainbow using mathematics and mathematical physics and produced experiments that led to how we understand light and color today.[124] Using a prism, he refracted white light (the pure white light that arrives from the sun) into its component colors of red, orange, yellow, green, blue, indigo, and violet, which make up the visible spectrum. His experiments showed that light was responsible for color, leading to the scientific study of color in nature and to breakthroughs in physics, chemistry, perception, and optics.

The sun's light is made up of electromagnetic waves of varying frequencies. When the mix of frequencies hits the eye at the same time, we see white, but when our eye catches a single, individual wave, we perceive a particular color. At one end of the spectrum are waves that we perceive as shades of violet; these are waves of frequencies between 670 and 780 THz (terahertz). At the other end, waves with frequencies between 400 and 480 THz are perceived as shades of red. Between the two are the other colors with varying frequencies.[125]

A mathematical explanation of a rainbow involves the basic geometry of lines and circles; for example, different refraction angles for the different frequencies of light give a rainbow its colors.[126] Most of us respond intuitively to its awe-inspiring beauty without understanding the mathematics that explain it.

## RECTANGLE AND PARALLELOGRAM

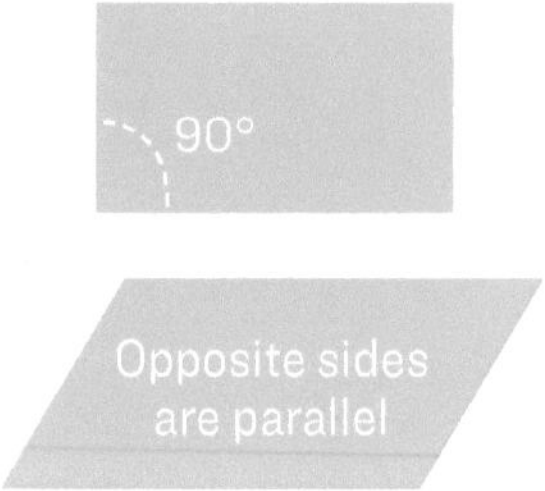

90°

Opposite sides are parallel

A rectangle is defined as a parallelogram that has four right angles. A parallelogram is a flat shape with four straight sides, the opposite sides of which are parallel to one another, equal in length, and with opposite angles that are also equal. (A square is another example of a parallelogram.)

SEE ALSO: **Square and Cube**

## RIGHT-HANDED EVOLUTION

**SEE CHIRALITY (p. 15)**

## RUDRAKSHA

Rudraksha is the name of an evergreen tree that grows in tropical and subtropical areas such as the Himalayas of Nepal and India; it is also the name given to its seeds. Tree and seeds are associated with Lord Shiva, the supreme being responsible for the cyclic creation, preservation, dissolution, and recreation of the universe; thus, in Eastern religions, according to Nibodhi Haas, "it is believed that the rudraksha contains secrets of the evolution of creation, as if mystically infused for the benefit of all human beings."[127] Used by Buddhists, Hindus, and Taoists, rudraksha may be worn on different parts of the body, placed nearby one's bedside or elsewhere if not worn, or taken internally in various forms and for different conditions to bring well-being on the material and spiritual levels. Among its many uses, it promotes peace of mind, brings prosperity, destroys negativities, and helps overcome obstacles and fear of an untimely death. It also bestows medicinal and astrological benefits. In India, it supports one's spiritual journey to lead one ultimately toward enlightenment and liberation, since wearing it pleases Lord Shiva and also the deities or divine cosmic energies that govern the nine planets of Vedic astrology. (Western science has recently removed Pluto from the nine planets of our solar system and reclassified it as a dwarf planet.)

*Mala of 54 rudraksha used by the author. Such a mala is counted twice (but in opposite directions to the Guru bead) to total 108.*

As well as having overall healing benefits, the spiritual power of rudraksha has to do with the number of facets or faces on a seed, as each number has particular healing qualities. The beads are strung into malas to be used in meditation and mantra chanting; the number of beads on a mala should be multiples of nine—27, 54, or 108—plus a single bead called the Guru bead.[128] All the numbers, including the one, are significant cosmologically.

SEE ALSO: **Buddhism; Hinduism; Mantra**

# SACRED GEOMETRY

Sacred geometry refers to the study of archetypal, original, and universal patterns of which the material world is composed and that are core patterns of creation.[129] Mathematics describes these patterns as "symmetrical." There exist many types of symmetries, but these are of a limited number in our universe as we know it.[130] These symmetries are found ubiquitously—in the natural world, in cultural expression, and even in the human mind. Author Mario Livio points out how symmetry "sits right at the intersection of science, art, and perceptual psychology, representing the stubborn cores of forms, laws, and mathematical objects that remain unchanged under transformations."[131]

> Sacred geometry "differs from mundane geometry purely in the sense that the moves and concepts involved are regarded as having symbolic value, and thus, like good music, facilitate the evolution of the soul."[132]
>
> —Miranda Lundy, *Sacred Geometry*

Symmetry has been proposed as a "theory of everything"[133] that unites science and culture. Underlying myth, mathematics, art, architecture, music, the financial world, the social sciences, psychology, the spiritual traditions, and more, it points toward the unification of symbolic meaning with mathematical manipulation, providing a comprehensive metaphor with which to describe processes of consciousness.

Scott Olsen suggests that consciousness itself may even reside in geometry, in the symmetry of the golden mean of DNA and other natural forms.[134] Such a metasystem links the individual, the group, and the universe.

Whereas science explains sacred geometry via physics and mathematics, many spiritual traditions, especially Indigenous traditions, are in sacred relationship with the universe and view its origin as metaphysical. In the words of Mircea Eliade, "The world is the work of Supernatural Beings—a divine work and hence sacred in its very structure."[135] Knowledge of any kind, including mathematical knowledge, is then acquired as sacred teaching.

SEE ALSO: **Cosmogenesis; Mathematics; Symmetry**

## SACRED SPACE

Everywhere in the world and far back in time, humans have created and consecrated places as spiritually significant. In both solitude and community, we do this for worship and ceremony, for celebration, healing, and spiritual initiation.

Human-made architecture—temples, churches, mosques—provide a space for close human/divine contact, bringing the divine nearer to humankind and our endeavors. The proportions, locations, ratios, forms, and measurements of sacred spaces are based on divine work because such formulas exist in nature. In Stephen Skinner's view, "Space is sacred when the geometry of its design depends on ratios that are either whole numbers or special, such as the Golden Mean. Sacred space looks and feels harmonious but also has an objective quality, which can be measured . . ."[136]

As an example, the Greek Parthenon, which was built around 450 BCE as a willing collective and not by enslaved people, was dedicated to the goddess Athena. It forms a perfect equilateral triangle in relation to two other temples when viewed from the sky.[137] Its fascinating history shows how the energy of a particular place may serve many purposes and traditions. Five centuries after the birth of Christianity, the Parthenon was closed down. Later it was converted into a Christian church. A thousand years after that, it became a mosque. Then in the early 19th century, half of its ornaments were sawed off by Lord Elgin and carried off to Britain (when that section of Greece was occupied by Turkey) and sold by Elgin in 1816 to the British government to pay off his extensive debts. During the German occupation of Athens, the Acropolis was made to fly a Nazi flag.

As a Siberian shaman expressed it, all of nature is sacred, but some places are more sacred than others. Places in nature, from caves and mountains to stones, trees, rivers, valleys, and other forms, become places of power and of sanctuary. Offerings may be made to a particular tree, a ceremony may be performed on a mountaintop to ask for protection, or shamans connecting with their helping spirits may draw on the walls of a cave.

In sacred space—natural or human-made—one enters the sublime from the everyday, the holy from the profane. Such places separate the linear and limited time of the physical world from the timelessness of the eternal to bring together heaven and earth. Such a relationship is expressed in many traditions as a square within a circle: The square represents earth, while the circle is the heavens, the unending and infinite, the One, and the repeating cycle of cosmic patterns.

SEE ALSO: Golden Mean; Mandala; Numbers; Shamanism

# SELF-ORGANIZATION

Scientists and naturalists are discovering more and more about the geometric patterns by which insects, plants, and other life-forms, along with bubbles, waves, and sand ripples on dunes, organize themselves. The process is called self-organization, or sometimes spontaneous order, referring "to the emergence of an overall order in time and space of a given system that results from the collective interactions of its individual components," in the words of Roland Wedlich-Söldner and Timo Betz.[138] The principle of self-organization is central to pattern formation in chemistry, physics, and biology.

SEE ALSO: Beehives and Honeycombs; Insects; Plants

# SHAMANISM

Although world religions have denigrated or even tried to eliminate shamanism, they have also integrated elements of it into their own beliefs and practices. Shamanism is the ancestral spiritual tradition of all peoples and cultures, going back in time to the origins of humanity.[139] Shamanic cultures are nature-based and in sacred relationship with the cosmos; the world is seen as a divine work and thus sacred in its very nature. Even innovations will be seen as revelations.[140] Ceremonies and rituals honor nature in all its diversity in song, dance, dress, and so on, as shamanists designate areas in the natural world as of particular spiritual significance, construct and organize their dwellings according to sacred principles, and pattern their social relationships on natural relationships.

Although sacred numbers are not restricted to these three in shamanist traditions, the numbers one, two, and three, and their multiples, are basic. The number three represents the tripartite universe of the Lower world, Middle world, and Upper world. All three need to be in balance for the universe to operate as it should. If not, a shaman will be called on to reinstate the natural order. The number two expresses the shamanic view of the world as a world of dualities. Nature itself is seen as dualistic: light/dark, heaven/earth, sun/moon, male/female, and so on. All is encompassed within the One—called the Creator, Source, Great Spirit, God, and other names in native languages that recognize the unity of all of creation.[141]

SEE ALSO: **Circle and Sphere; Numbers**

*Birchbark hat from Siberia showing circle motif, floral motifs, multiples of two and three, a center point, and a balance of light and dark, 2004.*

# SNOWFLAKES AND SNOW CRYSTALS

How many of us grew up thinking that every snowflake is unique? That's an interesting idea that is actually impossible to prove, although scientists think it is probably true. What snowflakes do have in common is their hexagonal shape. But what is a snowflake, anyway? Where do they come from?

Snowflake expert and physics professor Ken Libbrecht attributes the origin of snowflakes to droplets of moisture from a cloud in cold weather. When they freeze, they form tiny bits of ice that begin their meandering descent to earth. Because of the way water molecules fit together, the budding flakes form a lattice in the characteristic and familiar sixfold symmetrical shape of the hexagon.[142] But then other influences come into play.

German mathematician Harald Garcke points out how snowflakes form differently because of varying humidity and temperature conditions on their descent to earth and their differing paths due to the influence of wind. As other water condenses on the surface of the initial crystal, the characteristic hexagon forms. Eventually arms sprout and their shapes become more and more complicated. They may form needles, columns, or flat plates, while the sprouting arms may grow their own arms in a way that is similar to how branches form on a tree.[143]

Libbrecht suggests that we might want to distinguish between a snowflake and a snow crystal. The snow crystal is a single ice crystal showing that precise hexagonal structure.

*The sixfold symmetry of snowflakes.*

Though a snowflake can mean a snow crystal, it can also be used more generally to mean just about anything falling from winter clouds. Many, many falling snow crystals clump together in midair as they fall—hundreds or thousands of them—to form the fluffy puffballs we call snowflakes.

SEE ALSO: **Hexagon**

## SPIDERWEBS

Spiderwebs are astonishingly beautiful creations, and they are also marvels of engineering. Spider silks have been studied for their toughness, their structural integrity, their superior mechanical properties, and the way they optimize function. Such properties are found in the toughness of bone and the elasticity of blood vessels, among other natural materials that have been studied in relation to web geometry.[144] And

*Spiderwebs after rains, Nova Scotia, Canada.*

human engineers are adapting spider web geometry to human-designed architecture and other purposes.

Spiderwebs are spirals, but they are a particular type of spiral called Archimedean, which increases in size at a steady rate. The web is spun first as a framework and then filled in with spokes. From the center point, the spider then goes around and around, maintaining the same distance at each turn to produce the Archimedean spiral.

Scientists have found that spiders weave differing designs depending on the purpose of the web—to capture food, as housing, or as protection from predators. They can weave up to eight different types of silk depending on the purpose of the web. Web architecture is recognized as "a unique example in nature of high-performance material design," according to Isabelle Su.[145]

> *"Spiders build webs that are commonly several times their body size, with some exceptions such as the Darwin's bark spider* (Caerostris darwini) *that are capable of building webs that span rivers. The size of a spider web scaled up to human scale would be similar to the height of a multi-story building. While humans need bulky scaffolding or at least a crane to construct such a building, the spider only uses its silk."[146]*
> —Isabelle Su, et al., "Imaging and Analysis of a Three-Dimensional Spider Web Architecture"

SEE ALSO: **Spiral**

*Spiderwebs after rains,
Nova Scotia, Canada.*

# SPIRAL

In geometry, a spiral is defined as a plane curve produced by a point moving around a fixed point as it constantly recedes from or approaches it. It is one of nature's most common designs, found in the stars of a spiral galaxy, on the heads of daisies and sunflowers, and in the nautilus shell and pinecone. It has also captured the imaginations of countless cultures and spiritual traditions. There exist two types of spirals: Archimedean and logarithmic or equiangular.

Characteristic of a spider web, an Archimedean spiral increases in size at a steady rate, in comparison to an equiangular spiral, the coils of which increase in width from one turn to the next. A snail shell or ram's horn is a characteristic equiangular spiral, created as its outer edge surface grows faster than the inner while the overall shape of the shell or horn doesn't change. The shape is retained as the succession of chambers is added.

As with fractals, in most natural spirals a small part looks the same as a larger part. This repeating shape is called *logarithmic*. Logarithmic spirals, or partial ones, are found in mollusks, animal horns, claws, and talons as well as in so-called spiral galaxies such as the Milky Way, along with whirlpools, tornadoes, and cyclones. As Philip Ball writes, "In principle, a logarithmic spiral can go on curling inward or outward forever and its form would never change."[147]

Spirals may rotate clockwise or counterclockwise. For example, the vortex of a cyclone rotates counterclockwise in the Northern Hemisphere but clockwise in the Southern

*This image (See Buddhism, p. 11) also depicts spiral symbolism, shown here on the dancer's mask. The spiral motif suggests movement and also connects the wearer to the sky world.*

McKee Springs Petroglyph, Dinosaur National Monument, Utah and Colorado, showing spiral pattern.

Edible fiddlehead ferns in the spring before they unfurl, Nova Scotia, Canada.

Hemisphere; this effect occurs as a result of the earth's own rotation.

On a sunflower, which is commonly used to illustrate two-directional spirals, the circular arrangement of the flower's head consists of two sets of logarithmic spirals rotating in opposite directions,[148] resulting in a double spiral form. Also fascinating about sunflowers is that the spiral arrangements of florets and seeds follow the Fibonacci sequence.

More on sunflowers, which turn toward sunlight: This unique property has inspired scientists to develop solar panels made from rows of tiny artificial flowers. The material from which they're made causes the stem to bend and thus point the artificial flower toward the light.[149]

SEE ALSO: **Fibonacci Sequence; Helix; Spiderwebs; Symmetry**

*Logarithmic spirals on the head of a sunflower.*

# SQUARE AND CUBE

Regardless of their size, squares and cubes always have the same shapes and proportions; thus, in a spiritual sense, they may be said to represent eternity.

Squares within a circle are basic shapes of a mandala, among other representations of the sacred. In many traditions, earth represented as a square is enclosed within the timelessness of the eternal, which is represented as a circle; the two together represent the union of heaven and earth, of the sublime and the mundane.

Cubes are one of the simplest and most common shapes found in the cells of minerals and crystals; table salt is one

such example. Each face of the cube is a square. The earliest text of the Jewish Kabbalah uses the image of the cube of space to describe the initial structure of the entirety of creation: The image has six directions and may be envisioned as a basic cubic crystal.[150]

SEE ALSO: **Circle and Sphere; Mandala; Platonic Solids**

# STONE CIRCLES

Stone circles from ancient times still exist in many parts of the world. Theories abound as to their purpose, but we are beginning to understand that they surely had a spiritual or sacred purpose, connecting this physical world to the metaphysical realm.

Among the most famous is Stonehenge in England. Stonehenge is now thought by scientists to be an observatory, constructed to watch the sun, identify the longest day of the year, and predict lunar eclipses. It contains astounding lunar and solar calendars. Though its construction began about 4,500 years ago, it was built over a long period of time in stages by different people with different languages. Its central stone circle is a masterpiece of engineering: At dawn on June 21, the summer solstice, you can look from the center of the circle through its stone archway to what is called the heel stone (a huge rock that lies outside the circle) to view the rising sun.

Not as well known but equally fascinating is what has come to be known as "Canada's Stonehenge," a group of geometrically arranged stones in what is now southern Alberta. Archaeologist Gordon Freeman found parallels between these stones and Stonehenge as well as other sites in England and Wales. Built 5,000 years ago by the Oxbow people of North America's Great Plains, it is a vast sun temple and calendar so accurate it showed a deception in the Gregorian calendar that we use today. A medicine wheel structure forms part of it. Freeman is careful to point out the sacred nature of the entire site to the Indigenous People of the area, advocating for the site's protection and for recognition of their rights to maintain it as such.[151]

*Stone circle, Stonehenge, England.*

SEE ALSO: **Medicine Wheel**

# SYMMETRY

*The daisy displays an approximate rotational symmetry, meaning it looks about the same when rotated by any angle.*

The order and regularity of pattern formation is a universal—in nature and in culture—and it bridges the so-called living and nonliving worlds. The concept of symmetry can describe such universals and is thus termed the basic scientific "language" of form and pattern. Symmetry expresses a sense of an orderly cosmos and reveals a kind of spontaneous creativity in nature,[152] whether attributed to a divine power or to the laws of science and whether viewed at the macro level—as in the arrangement of the planets in the cosmos—or at the micro level—as in the structure of a bacteria or slime mold that can only be seen through a microscope or via computational tools.

The word *symmetry* comes from the Greek *sym* and *metria* meaning "the same measure" and originally had to do with proportion and its ensuing beauty. In the 18th century, it was introduced to mean "immunity to a possible change" in the mathematical sense. Group theory, the branch of mathematics dealing with groups, is recognized today as "the mathematical language that describes the essence of symmetries and explores their properties," according to astrophysicist Mario Livio.[153]

Livio describes the fundamental role of symmetry in nature and its impact on the development of science:

> *"With every step toward the revolutions of relativity and quantum mechanics, the role of symmetry in the laws of nature has become increasingly appreciated. Physicists are no longer*

> *content with finding explanations for individual phenomena. Rather, they are now convinced more than ever that nature has an underlying design in which symmetry is the key ingredient ... symmetry is one of the most important tools in deciphering nature's design."* [154]

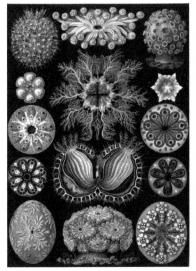  

*Illustrations of various life-forms showing their symmetry and intrinsic beauty by German biologist Ernst Haeckel in his book* Kunstformen der Natur *(published in English as* Art Forms in Nature*), first published between 1899 and 1904.*

Although perhaps appearing chaotic to the casual observer, nature produces both symmetry and "symmetry-breaking," or the partial destruction of symmetry that turns things that are the same into things that are different: "The more symmetry that gets broken, the more subtle and elaborate the pattern," according to Philip Ball.[155] Symmetry-breaking appears in the ripples of sand that form on the seashore and in the waves

*Religious symbols incorporating a variety of symmetries.*

on the sea's surface. On the grand scale it may be the impetus for evolution.

Humans have incorporated nature's symmetry into architecture, art, music, and even language and other forms of cultural expression.

Twentieth-century psychologists Carl Jung[156] and Robert A. Johnson[157] viewed symmetry as fundamental to their healing practices. The archetype is associated with Jung, but it had been around for much longer, going back at least as far as Plato and others. In Platonic terms, archetypes refer to the unseen fundamentals from which objects and images manifest in the material world. Jung viewed archetypes similarly: "Eternal ideas are primordial images stored up (in a supracelestial place) as eternal, transcendent forms."[158] Archetypes also have numinous or spiritual qualities. Out of this original order, the psyche emerges, as do all other symmetrical manifestations, nature-based and human-made.

Johnson, describing this Jungian concept of "self," writes that the awakening of the *symmetrical* unity of the self is the great goal of our psychological evolution: "The *self* is the sum of all the divergent forces, energies, and qualities that live within you and make you who you are—a unique individual. The self is the balanced, harmonious, symmetrical unity at the very center of one's being, which each of us senses within."[159]

Mario Livio uses symmetry to explain and understand the underlying structure and order of the natural and human-made worlds. He discusses how symmetry has become a pivotal concept "in our ideas about the cosmos around us and in the fundamental theories attempting to explain it"[160] and is a crucial aesthetic element. Symmetric pattern also provokes intense emotional response. There is even a preference for symmetry in animal mate selection.

Livio identifies a definitive quantity of symmetries in our cosmos: "There exist only 230 different types of spatial symmetry groups (just as there are only 7 different symmetry groups of linear strip patterns)."[161] These include the familiar bilateral symmetry, also called mirror-reflection symmetry (up/down, front/back, etc.), that is characteristic of the human body, as well as rotation, reflection, translation (meaning a movement in a particular direction), and glide reflection symmetries. Rotational symmetry is characteristic of snowflakes, whereas the circle is one of the simplest rotationally symmetric figures. Symmetries may be combined, as with glide-reflection symmetry, which is as a combination of translation and reflection symmetry; footprints generated by an alternating left-right-left-right walk exhibit glide-reflection symmetry.

SEE ALSO: Bird Flight; Churches; Circle and Sphere; da Vinci, Leonardo; Helix; Plato; Snowflakes and Snow Crystals

# THEORY OF RELATIVITY

Albert Einstein's theory of relativity, also known as general relativity, is a geometric theory of gravitation that he published in 1915 and that has become the explanation of gravitation by modern physics. It states that space and time are not constants; they are relative. Einstein predicted, for example, that the higher the elevation, the more quickly time passes, as in the example of two clocks positioned a foot apart in height above sea level. The increased gravitational pull of a clock closer to the center of a planet such as Earth causes time to move more slowly than the clock placed above. Time can also slow down or speed up depending on the position and speed of the observer. Relativity theory—and its modification of earlier scientific concepts of time and space as fixed and absolute—"was therefore one of the greatest revolutions in the history of science," according to Fritjof Capra, affecting not just science but also philosophy, spirituality, and how we view nature. Geometry, in this view, "is not inherent in nature, but is imposed upon it by the mind." Measurement is thus not "real." A shadow, for example, is a projection of points in three-dimensional space onto a two-dimensional plane; thus, its length will differ based on different angles of projection.[162]

SEE ALSO: **Dimension; Eastern Mysticism and Physics**

# TOPOLOGY

In mathematics, topology is the study of those properties of a geometric object that are retained through deformations such as twisting, stretching, bending, and crumpling (but not tearing or dissembling). Thus, for example, a circle may be stretched into an ellipse. The only major branch of modern mathematics that was not foreseen by ancient mathematicians, it was once considered to be limited to abstract mathematics without applications. In more recent studies, topology is applied to understanding real-world phenomena such as evolution and disease and the relationship between topology and liquid crystals.[163]

SEE ALSO: **Ellipse**

# TREE OF LIFE

The cosmic tree, world tree, tree of life, or axis mundi is an archetype that seems universal across cultures and religions, symbolizing strength, growth, fertility, and nourishment as well as spiritual transformation and resurrection. For example, it represents the three worlds of shamanism's tripartite universe: The branches are the Upper world, the trunk is the Middle world, and the roots are the Lower world. Trees are entry points for shamans to enter the other worlds: By climbing a tree, a shaman ascends to the heavens or sky world; by journeying into the roots of the tree, a shaman descends into the lower world.[164] It is common to find images of birds atop a tree (or a pole, which is a tree stripped of its branches), which represent the shaman's soul in flight. In some Christian traditions, the tree of life becomes the cross of Christ's crucifixion, while Christmas is celebrated with a Christmas tree (usually a conifer). In the Buddhist tradition, Buddha reached enlightenment sitting under a bodhi tree. In sacred geometry, the tree is often used to illustrate fractals.

SEE ALSO: **Buddhism; Fractal; Shamanism**

*Yggdrasil is an immense ash tree central to Norse cosmology and is considered very holy. From a plate included in the English translation of the* Prose Edda *by Oluf Olufsen Bagge (1847).*

# TRIANGLE AND PYRAMID

Simply put, a triangle is three points joined together (but not all on the same line). It is a fundamental geometrical form and the most stable due to the sum of its three internal angles, which always equals 180 degrees or half of a circle. In nature, the triangular form is ubiquitous and exists on every scale from the minute to the cosmic, including as fractals. Rock formations, flower petals, and so many other elements in nature are based on the triangle. Though there are many possible triangles, the three most common have been used regularly in architecture and also in mapping: the equilateral, the isosceles, and the right-angled. They are also the building blocks for other geometrical forms, including the pyramid.

The outer surfaces of a pyramid, of which there are at least three (plus the base), are triangular and converge at the top, while the base of a pyramid can be trilateral, quadrilateral, or of any polygon shape. The common square pyramid has a square base and four triangular outer surfaces. A pyramid with a triangular base is called a tetrahedron. Two identical, square-based pyramids joined together at their bases are called an octahedron. Pyramid geometry, especially the geometry of the Egyptian pyramids, has fascinated mathematicians for millennia.

SEE ALSO: **Ancient Egypt; Fractal; Platonic Solids; Polygon**

*Fractals and triangles in mountains and rock formations (Top: Capitol Reef National Park, Utah; Bottom: The Lut Desert, Iran).*

# TRIPARTITE UNIVERSE

Many cultures portray the universe as a trinity or triad, that is, as tripartite, meaning "of three parts." In Christianity, for example, the universe is made up of heaven, earth, and hell; in shamanic traditions, of the Upper, Middle, and Lower worlds.[165] Trees seem to be a universal, nature-based representation of the tripartite universe. In these two traditions, respectively, the roots represent the Lower world, or hell; the trunk represents the Middle world, or earth; and the branches represent the Upper world, or heaven.

Eastern religions portray the three levels in the powerful symbol of OM, which means this eternal world is all—what was, what is, and what shall be. In the Sanskrit letter for OM (see page 72), the lower curve stands for the dream state, the curve extending out from the center stands for deep, dreamless sleep, and the upper curve stands for the waking state. Above these three states, the crescent stands for the veil of illusion, and the single dot stands for the state of transcendence. When one's spirit passes through the veil to rest in transcendence, one is liberated from the three states and their qualities and limitations.

The three-sided equilateral triangle consists of equal sides and angles. As such, it appears in much religious and spiritual art as the basic structure of the universe, representing balance, harmony, and relationship among the three worlds.

SEE ALSO: **Numbers; Mantra; Shamanism; Triangle and Pyramid**

# TRIVIUM

Seven liberal arts subjects formed the basis of the monastic system of education in medieval times. These were composed of the trivium and the quadrivium. The term *trivium* comes from the Latin *tri* and *via*; it translates as "the place where three roads meet." Grammar, logic, and rhetoric comprised the three verbal or language arts of the trivium. Grammar ensured proper structure of language. Logic was for arriving at the truth. Rhetoric taught the beautiful use of language; thus, the trivium incorporated the three essentials of goodness, truth, and beauty.[166] As an introductory curriculum, the trivium prepared students for the quadrivium.

SEE ALSO: **Music; Quadrivium**

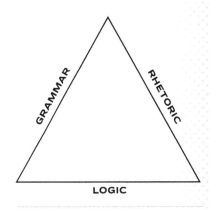

*Trivium.*

# TWO-DIMENSIONAL AND THREE-DIMENSIONAL GEOMETRY

Two-dimensional geometry, or planar geometry, is based on the idea that, for a given point on a line, only one perpendicular line exists. Thus, a two-dimensional shape has only two measurements such as width and height (and no thickness). Three-dimensional geometry, in comparison, is based on the idea that there exist an infinite number of lines that are perpendicular to a given line, and a three-dimensional shape has three measurements, such as width, height, and length.

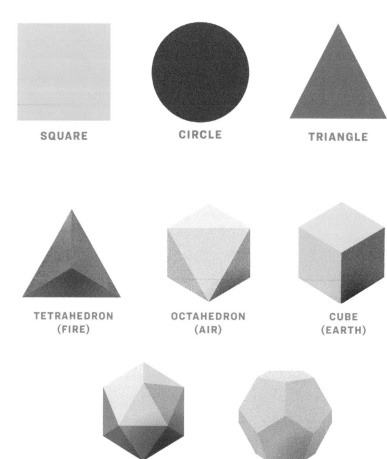

*Examples of two-dimensional shapes.*

SQUARE

CIRCLE

TRIANGLE

TETRAHEDRON
(FIRE)

OCTAHEDRON
(AIR)

CUBE
(EARTH)

ICOSAHEDRON
(WATER)

DODECAHEDRON
(ETHER)

*Examples of three-dimensional shapes.*

The five examples of three-dimensional shapes shown here are known as the five regular three-dimensional solids, also called the five Platonic solids. Although named after Plato, they existed at least 2,000 years earlier, having been found as full sets at Neolithic stone circles in Aberdeenshire, Scotland.[167] As basic shapes that underlie the entirety of observable reality, they are also called the five elements found in nature, which many spiritual and healing traditions—Ayurveda and Buddhism among them—recognize and on which they base their practice.

Science also discusses dimensions higher than three: "Higher dimensional geometries and spaces are those with a dimension greater than three. These are beyond our perception, since we can move forward and backward, to the left and right, and up and down in the space were [sic] we live. *Time* could be considered a possible fourth dimension, but we have no sense to perceive time," according to the proceedings of a 2018 conference on geometry.[168]

SEE ALSO: Buddhism; Dimension; Flower of Life; Plato; Platonic Solids; Stone Circles

# UNIVERSE

The word *universe* derives from the Old French word *univers*, which in turn derives from the Latin *universum* meaning "whole, entire." The universe, also called the cosmos, is thus the entirety of space and all it contains—stars, planets, and other forms of energy and matter.

Galactic experts at the University of Montreal, Canada, who researched almost 1,000 planets, discovered that planets in star systems form in the same shape pattern: "Every planet in a system is close in size and similarly spaced in its orbit in comparison with planets in other systems."[169] Such a finding challenges our understanding of how systems form. At the same time, it advances scientific understanding of the mysteries of our universe, its origins, and how it operates. Yet geometry and symmetry appear to underlie its structure and evolution; astronomer Mario Livio, for example, discusses the limited number of symmetries of which our universe—its natural and human-made worlds—is composed.[170]

A fascinating question occupies scientists now, what some are calling a "cosmological crisis" because of challenges to our current understanding of the cosmos: Is the universe spherical or flat? If the universe is spherical, it is "closed," which would mean that if you traveled far enough in the universe, you could end up back where you started. But if the large-scale appearance of the universe is a flat sheet, or at least very close to being flat, then it would have infinite extension and could go on forever without coming back to itself. Either way offers no definitive answer, and so the mystery remains.

# VANISHING POINT AND PERSPECTIVE

The rules of linear perspective and the incorporation of the vanishing point are relatively new in the development of arts and architecture but are now universally accepted. Perspective is the application of optical knowledge to suggest depth in flat paintings and drawings or to convey increased depth in low-relief sculpture, whereas the vanishing point—a single focus in an artwork—means that all parallel lines converge.

The discovery of perspective and vanishing point goes back to Italian Renaissance architect and designer Filippo Brunelleschi. Using two mathematical principles, Brunelleschi was able to calculate the relationship between an object's actual length and its visual length in a painting, which depended on its distance from the viewer.

Later, Italian mathematician, author, and artist Piero Della Francesca incorporated perspective and geometric forms into his paintings of Christ, the Nativity, and other religious subjects. His influence on the work of Fra Luca Bartolomeo de Pacioli, an Italian mathematician and Franciscan friar who collaborated with Leonardo da Vinci, led to the development of formulas for finding the exact relationship between the distance from the eye to the object and the object's size in the picture.

> "The Ancients, having taken into consideration the rigorous construction of the human body, elaborated all their works, as especially their holy temples, according to these proportions."[171]
> —Luca Pacioli, *De Divina Proportione*, June 1, 1509

SEE ALSO: **Circle and Sphere; da Vinci, Leonardo; Square and Cube**

# VĀSTU ŚĀSTRA

Vāstu Śāstra (vastu shastra) is the Indian art and science, derived from the Vedas, concerned with the positioning of objects with the intent to divert the flow of negative energy and harness the flow of positive energy. As such, it is similar to Chinese feng shui. Basic premises are that every object exerts an influence on the mind,[172] that the laws of nature affect human dwellings and activities, and that living beings and their natural environments need to be in proper alignment. It incorporates symmetry, geometric patterns known as yantras, and directional alignments.

Once applied mainly to Hindu architecture, especially Hindu temples, Vāstu Śāstra developed broad applications to architectural and building principles, interior design, landscaping, dance, poetry, sculpture, painting, and many other fields. A sacred practice, it structures and maintains our physical environment for maximum happiness and well-being, teaching us to live in harmony both within and without.

SEE ALSO: **Feng Shui; Vedas; Yantra**

# VEDAS

The Vedas are the most ancient of all the scriptures of Hinduism and the oldest texts in Sanskrit. According to Hinduism, they were not actually composed by anyone, and no author is credited with them; instead, it is believed that they were revealed to the ancient rishis (self-realized seers or sages) during deep meditation and are thus apauruṣeya, which means authorless, impersonal, and "not of a person" or super-human. The mantras that compose the Vedas are said to have always existed in nature in the form of subtle vibrations, and while the rishis were so deeply absorbed in their practice, they were able to perceive the mantras.[173]

The Vedas are believed to date to sometime between 1500 and 1000 BCE in what is now Pakistan and northwest India. They were passed down orally over many generations until parts were transcribed at different times. It is believed, however, that the entire collection was completed by the end of the second millennium BCE.[174] Copies of only two of the earliest known Vedas have survived the passages of time and are held in the Bhandarkar Oriental Institute in India.

SEE ALSO: **Hinduism; Mantra**

# VESICA PISCIS

The term *vesica piscis* comes from Latin, meaning "bladder of a fish," as it looks like the joined dual air bladders of most fish. A vesica is also called a mandorla, which translates to "almond." A vesica piscis is the almond-shaped center of two intersecting and overlapping circles of the same radius, with each centered on the edge of the other. It appears in many cultures throughout time from the geometric design of Hindu temples to modern-day corporate logos. In Christianity, it symbolizes the coming together of heaven and earth through Jesus. In Muslim arches and cathedral doorways, it may

*Vesica piscis illustrating lines, triangles, and circles.*

be said to represent the passing from the mundane into the spiritual.

In nature, a stoma (plural *stomata*) on the underside of a leaf forms an almond-shaped opening as pairs of guard cells open and close to allow for gas exchange. Two pebbles dropped into a pond at some distance apart will produce intersecting rings, at the center of which will be a vesica piscis.

In mathematics, the vesica piscis is the basis of the proportions that generate polygons and the five Platonic solids as well as the triangle, the square, the pentagon, and all the shapes they form. In sacred geometry, it symbolizes the central and ultimate "oneness" created by the union of pairs or opposites.

SEE ALSO: **Flower of Life; Plants; Platonic Solids; Polygon**

# VORTEX

In lay terms, a vortex is a swirling mass of water that involves suction (such as a whirlpool) or of air that takes shape as a column or spiral (such as a tornado). Water draining down a sink or bathtub or a flushing toilet exhibits the same processes as air forming into a tornado. A drain's whirlpool, which is also known as a vortex, forms because the drain creates a downdraft in water. The water's downward flow into the drain begins to rotate or spiral, and the rotation increases in speed, forming a vortex. Vortices are common in nature, from dust devils in the desert to fire whirls, which are climbing vortices of flame and ash occurring in wildfires. On the cosmic scale, scientists have noted dust devils on Mars as well as what they call solar tornadoes whipping out from the sun.[175] Tornadoes that occur on Earth are incomparable to the monstrous solar tornadoes, which are magnetic events involving super-heated solar gases swirling deep within the atmosphere of the sun. They spin at a speed of up to 190,000 miles per hour and measure more than the width of several Earths in size.[176]

SEE ALSO: **Spiral**

# WATER

Water is a simple molecule consisting of one oxygen atom bonded to two different hydrogen atoms, resulting in an approximate tetrahedral geometry around each oxygen atom.[177] Water is thus conditioned by geometry even though it is fluid. When water cools, energy is taken out of it as its molecular motion slows down. Water then freezes into ice, a solid. As it does so, its density gradually decreases, and the hydrogen bonds start to form a network in a structure that is generally made up of hexagons (six-sided polygons) with open spaces in their centers. In ice, too, each water molecule bonds with its nearest neighbors to form a perfect tetrahedron, or three-sided pyramid, which comprises the most basic molecular geometry of water and may be the most basic structure of the universe.[178] Moving water takes on a variety of shapes. Meandering water in the form of a river, for example, exhibits a particular geometry depending on its volume and silt load, while whirlpools assume the geometry of a spiral. Water droplets are shaped by forces such as surface tension and gravity; they will be more or less spherical or lens-shaped or may even out into a thin film.

SEE ALSO: **Atom; The Hidden Messages in Water; Molecule; Polygon; Spiral; Triangle and Pyramid**

# YANTRA

In Hinduism, a yantra is a power diagram, a geometrical composition of abstract symbols. It is a dynamic representation, the power of which increases in proportion to its level of abstraction and precision.[179] Yantras serve a number of purposes in architecture, art, astronomy, physics, and other fields. They are applied to temple plans; can serve as meditation tools to increase awareness and support an individual's spiritual journey; or may be used as magical devices to, for instance, alter the energy of a place. Particular deities in the Hindu pantheon—Kali, Vishnu, Shiva, and so on—have their own yantra in which the deity is an abstraction of its essence rather than an anthropomorphic image.

Yantras are archetypes that reveal the basic constructions of which the universe is composed. They are built from four shapes—the point, triangle, square, and circle—each of which may have multiple interpretations. These shapes function as "thought forms" that embody particular patterns of force that can be heard in the sound-syllable of the yantra's corresponding mantra; yantras are considered to be "ensouled" by mantra. According to Madhu Khanna, identifying with the pattern is to "realize or release the inherent forces that each form denotes."[180]

> "Together, yantra-mantra may be said to build form *(by the act of configuration)*, to conserve form *(the configuration itself)*, and finally to dissolve form *(as the aspirant comprehends its inner meaning and soars beyond it)*."[181]
>
> —Madhu Khanna, *Yantra: The Tantric Symbol of Cosmic Unity*

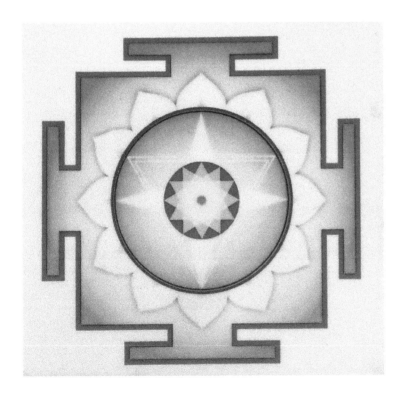

*The rays emerging from this yantra will remove negativity in dwellings of all types and bestow auspiciousness. Created with the blessings of Śri Mata Amritanandamayi Devi.*

SEE ALSO: **Hinduism; Mantra**

# YURT

*Yurt camp, Mongolia, 2007.*

*Yurt roof showing central circle, Mongolia, 2009.*

The domed or sometimes conical yurt (also called a ger) is the traditional dwelling of Siberian and Mongolian nomadic herders. Like the Inuit snow house of the Arctic, its shape provides minimum exposed surface and maximum stability to suit a migratory lifestyle. As with other forms of Indigenous architecture, the yurt is constructed according to geometric principles derived from nature. Made of wooden slats, the frame is a collapsible lattice-like structure that folds up, accordion-style, for easy transport. The wool covering is felted from their herd animals (sheep, goat, yak, camel, or horse) and laid over the frame as the roof and walls. The same structure is used year-round, with the felt acting as effective insulation to keep the heat in during the cold months and provide shade from the hot sun in the summer months. On hot summer days, the felt walls are rolled from ground level up and tied for ventilation, and the door is left open. For cold summer nights after the sun has set, the felt is easily rolled back down. And wool retains its insulative properties even when wet, so it weathers rain and snow. The ingenuity of this framework allows a yurt to be set up or taken down within half an hour. The open interior allows for multiple uses; thus, spiritual and mundane activities are not separated.

An orthographic view of a yurt reveals it to be a circle. The circular design is important structurally and spiritually, with no corners where energies might become trapped and where energy moves smoothly around the circumference. Forming a cartwheel, six spokes meet at the center circle of the roof. This center circle is supported by two slender posts, which fix into sockets and extend to be supported by the lattice of the yurt wall. The stove, sometimes with an attached chimney, is located between the roof posts at the center of the interior. It is the nexus of the yurt, the central and most important point or place. The rising smoke escapes between the spokes of the sacred circle above. (The ceiling hole can be covered or opened from inside by means of a long pole to expel or retain heat.)

Sacred plants, such as juniper or cedar, are burned as incense on the stovetop. The smoke travels upward to exit through the center circle, connecting people in this world with their ancestors in the spirit world who provide protection and guidance. In his novel *The Blue Sky*, Galsan Tschinag, a Mongolian shaman of Tuvan ancestry, writes how the sky, in the shamanist tradition, is the resting place of the spirits and is master of all things in the universe.[182] The circle in the roof thus acts as a portal that invites, locates, and integrates the physical and metaphysical realms to harmonize the universe.

The layout is generally based on the four directions: north, east, south, and west. The hearth separates the women's place from the men's, and family from visitor, dividing the space into fours. As a visitor, it is extremely disrespectful to sit with your feet pointing toward the sacred space at the rear of the yurt or to cross in front of it from behind the stove. Buddhism has become the official religion of Mongolia now, but many Mongolians and Siberians still practice shamanism as their ancestral spirituality. Both can be accommodated in the traditional yurt layout. Photographs of deceased family members and offerings to the spirits, such as wrapped candies, along with other Buddhist or shamanic objects (and sometimes both) are placed on an altar located at the back, across from the entrance. The entrance will face east or sometimes south, so that when you exit in the morning, you greet the sun as the source of all life. Thus, the yurt offers visual instruction about spiritual truths and gives physical form to metaphysical insight. As a model of the cosmos, the yurt acts as a sort of blueprint for the ecological, aesthetic, social, and cosmological relations that are both shaped by and reflected in the built environment.[183]

SEE ALSO: **Circle and Sphere; Shamanism**

# ZEN

## SEE JAPANESE GARDENS (p. 64)

# ZODIAC

In astronomy and astrology, the zodiac is a band of the celestial sphere. It extends about eight or nine degrees on either side of the ecliptic, which is the plane of the earth's orbit and of the sun's apparent annual path. It represents the portion of the sky within which the paths of the sun, the moon, and the planets are located.

Known generally as a band of 12 celestial constellations, it has been viewed as a timepiece or calendar with the system of planets and constellations emerging from elementary geometric patterns.[184] Most systems use these 12 astrological signs: Aries, Taurus, Gemini, Cancer, Leo, Virgo, Libra, Scorpio, Sagittarius, Capricorn, Aquarius, and Pisces.

*Zodiac wheel with symbols representing the 12 signs. From top (clockwise): Aries, Pisces, Aquarius, Capricorn, Sagittarius, Scorpio, Libra, Virgo, Leo, Cancer, Gemini, and Taurus.*

SEE ALSO: **Astrology; Geometry**

# NOTES

1 Swami Purnamritananda Puri, *Unforgettable Memories* (Kerala, India: Mata Amritanandamayi Mission Trust, 2008), 170.

2 Michael Brooks, "Is the Universe Conscious? It Sounds Implausible. But That's Until You Do the Math," *New Scientist* (May 2–8, 2020): 40–44.

3 Marilyn Walker, *Shamanism: An A–Z Reference Guide; Beliefs and Practices from around the World* (Emeryville, CA: Rockridge Press, 2020).

4 Marcia Wendorf, "Ancient Egyptian Technology and Inventions," *Interesting Engineering*, April 23, 2019, interestingengineering.com/ancient -egyptian-technology-and-inventions.

5 *Encyclopaedia Britannica*, "Mathematics in Ancient Egypt," accessed July 28, 2020, britannica.com/science/mathematics /Mathematics-in-ancient-Egypt.

6 *ScienceDaily*, "How Were the Egyptian Pyramids Built?" March 29, 2008, sciencedaily.com/releases/2008/03 /080328104302.htm.

7 William L. Hosch, ed., *The Britannica Guide to Geometry* (Chicago: Britannica Educational Publishing, 2011).

8 *Merriam-Webster.com Dictionary*, s.v. "Area," accessed April 16, 2020, merriam-webster.com/dictionary/area.

9 Steven Scott Pither, *The Complete Book of Numbers: The Power of Number Symbols to*

*Shape Reality* (St. Paul, MN: Llewellyn Publications, 2002), 1.

10  Men-Tsee-Khang (The Tibetan and Astrological Institute of H.H. the Dalai Lama), *Tibetan Astronomy and Astrology: An Introduction* (Dharamsala, India: Men-Tsee-Khang, 2001), 9–10.

11  Elizabeth Landau, "10 Things Einstein Got Right," *NASA Science: Solar System Exploration*, May 29, 2019, solarsystem .nasa.gov/news/954/10-things-einstein -got-right.

12  Ali Sundermier, "The Particle Physics of You," *Symmetry*, November 3, 2015, symmetrymagazine.org/article/the -particle-physics-of-you.

13  "Binary Number System," *MathIsFun .com*, accessed July 28, 2020, mathsisfun .com/binary-number-system.html.

14  Bret W. Tobalske, "Biomechanics of Bird Flight," *Journal of Experimental Biology* 210 (2007): 3135–46, doi.org/10.1242/jeb .000273.

15  "Line Symmetry in Birds," *All about Symmetry*, accessed July 28, 2020, all-about-symmetry.com/line -symmetry-birds.

16  J. R. Santiago, *Sacred Symbols of Buddhism* (Delhi: Book Faith India, 1999).

17  *Definitions.net*, s.v. "Capella," accessed July 28, 2020, definitions.net/definition /Capella.

18  Walker, *Shamanism*.

19  Armin Haupt and Nicolas Minc, "How Cells Sense Their Own Shape: Mechanisms to Probe Cell Geometry and Their Implications in Cellular Organization and Function," *Journal of Cell Science* 131 (March 26, 2018), doi.org/10.1242 /jcs.214015.

20  Lama Anagarika Govinda, *Foundations of Tibetan Mysticism: According to the Esoteric Teachings of the Great Mantra OM MANI PADME HŪM* (York Beach, ME: Samuel Weiser, 1989), 124.

21  Roger A. Hegstrom and Dilip K. Kondepudi, "The Handedness of the Universe," *Scientific American* 262, no. 1 (January 1990), 108–15, doi.org/10.1038 /scientificamerican0190-108.

22 David Wade, *Symmetry: The Ordering Principle* (Wiltshire, England: Wooden Books, 2006), 24.

23 Margaret Visser, *The Geometry of Love: Space, Time, Mystery, and Meaning in an Ordinary Church* (New York: North Point Press, 2002), 4–5.

24 Johannes Kepler, *Harmonies of the World*, trans. Charles Glenn Wallis (CreateSpace Independent Publishing Platform, 2014).

25 Wassim Jabi and Iakovos Potamianos, "Geometry, Light, and Cosmology in the Church of Hagia Sophia," *International Journal of Architectural Computing* 5, no. 2 (2007): 303–19, doi.org/10.1260/1478-0771.5.2.304.

26 Hosch, *Britannica Guide to Geometry*.

27 Marilyn Walker, "Circumpolar Shelter," in *Architecture* (Arctic Perspective Cahier, No. 1), ed. Andreas Muller (Hartware, Germany: Hatje Cantz), 60–81.

28 Mircea Eliade, *Rights and Symbols of Initiation: The Mysteries of Birth and Rebirth*, trans. W. Trask (London: Harvill Press, 1958), xii.

29 Michio Kaku and Jennifer Thompson, *Beyond Einstein* (Oxford, England: Oxford University Press, 1987), 5–6.

30 Jon Cartwright, "Welcome to the Antiverse: Mysterious Particles Uncovered in the Antarctic Could Be Evidence of a Mind-Bending Mirror Universe," *New Scientist*, April 11, 2020, 34–38.

31 Cartwright, "Welcome to the Antiverse," 34–38.

32 David L. Bryce and Francis Taulelle, "NMR Crystallography," *Acta Crystallographica Section C* 73, no. 3 (March 2017), 126–27, doi.org/10.1107/S2053229617001589.

33 Philip Ball, *Patterns in Nature: Why the Natural World Looks the Way It Does* (Chicago: The University of Chicago Press, 2016), 190.

34 Hans Jenny, "Cymatics: The Sculpture of Vibrations," *The UNESCO Courier: A Window Open on the World* XXII, no. 12 (1969): 4–31, unesdoc.unesco.org/ark:/48223/pf0000058744.

35 Serge Bramly, *Discovering the Life of Leonardo da Vinci: A Biography* (New York: Edward Burlingame Books, 1991).

36 Bramly, *Discovering the Life*, 275.

37 "The Vitruvian Man," *LeonardoDaVinci.net*, accessed July 28, 2020, leonardodavinci.net/the-vitruvian-man.jsp.

38 "Famous Leonardo DaVinci's Quotes," *LeonardoDaVinci.net*, accessed July 28, 2020, leonardodavinci.net/quotes.jsp.

39 Bramly, *Discovering the Life*.

40 Luca Pacioli, *De Divina Proportione*, with illustrations by Leonardo da Vinci, published online August 22, 2011, issuu.com/s.c.williams-library/docs/de_divina_proportione.

41 Hosch, *Britannica Guide to Geometry*.

42 Nicholas Clauvelin, Wilma K. Olson, and Irwin Tobias, "Characterization of the Geometry and Topology of DNA Pictured as a Discrete Collection of Atoms," *Journal of Chemical Theory and Computation* 8, no. 3 (2012): 1092–1107, doi.org/10.1021/ct200657e.

43 Hosch, *Britannica Guide to Geometry*.

44 Walker, *Shamanism*.

45 Fritjof Capra, *The Tao of Physics: An Exploration of the Parallels between Modern Physics and Eastern Mysticism* (London: Wildwood House, 1975), 180.

46 *Merriam-Webster.com Dictionary*, s.v. "Ellipse," accessed July 28, 2020, merriam-webster.com/dictionary/ellipse.

47 David Berlinski, *The King of Infinite Space: Euclid and His Elements* (New York: Basic Books, 2013).

48 Stephen Skinner, *Guide to Feng Shui* (New York: DK Publishing, 2001), 27.

49 *The Fibonacci Association*, accessed July 28, 2020, mathstat.dal.ca/fibonacci.

50 Ball, *Patterns in Nature*, 82.

51 Ron Knott, "Fibonacci Numbers and Nature," accessed July 28, 2020, maths.surrey.ac.uk/hosted-sites/R.Knott/Fibonacci/fib.html.

52 Sudipta Sinha, "The Fibonacci Numbers and Its Amazing Applications," *International Journal of Engineering Science Invention* 6, no. 9 (September 2017): 7–14.

53  William Blake, "Auguries of Innocence," *Poets.org*, accessed July 28, 2020, poets.org/poem/auguries-innocence.

54  Ball, *Patterns in Nature*, 48.

55  Ball, *Patterns in Nature*, 54.

56  Jordana Cepelewicz, "Is Consciousness Fractal?," *Nautilus*, May 4, 2017, nautil.us/issue/47/consciousness/is-consciousness-fractal.

57  Cepelewicz, "Is Consciousness Fractal?"

58  Mario Livio, *The Equation That Couldn't Be Solved: How Mathematical Genius Discovered the Language of Symmetry* (New York: Simon and Schuster, 2005).

59  Livio, *Equation*, 21.

60  Jeremy Narby, *The Cosmic Serpent: DNA and the Origins of Knowledge* (New York: Jeremy P. Tarcher/Putnam, 1998).

61  *Dictionary.com*, s.v. "Hexagram," accessed July 28, 2020, dictionary.com/browse/hexagram.

62  Puri, *Unforgettable Memories*.

63  Swami Jnanamritananda, ed., *Lead Us to the Light: A Collection of Mata Amritanandamayi's Teachings* (San Ramon, CA: Mata Amritanandamayi Center, 2002).

64  Tim Hinchliffe, "New Evidence for Holographic Universe Backs Up Ancient Esoteric Teachings," *The Sociable*, February 2, 2017, sociable.co/technology/holographic-universe-ancient-philosophy.

65  Ken Wilbur, ed., *The Holographic Paradigm and Other Paradoxes* (Boulder, CO: Shambala Press, 1982), 2.

66  Coleman Barks, *Rumi: The Book of Love: Poems of Ecstasy and Longing* (New York: HarperCollins, 2005).

67  Niayesh Afshordi et al., "From Planck Data to Planck Era: Observational Tests of Holographic Cosmology," *Physical Review Letters* 118 (January 27, 2017), doi.org/10.1103/PhysRevLett.118.041301.

68  David Bohm, *Wholeness and the Implicate Order* (London: Routledge and Kegan Paul, 1980).

69 Michael Talbot, *The Holographic Universe* (London: HarperCollins, 1991).

70 Danah Zohar, *The Quantum Self* (New York: Quill/William Morrow, 1990).

71 *Encyclopaedia Britannica*, s.v. "Iamblichus," accessed July 28, 2020, britannica.com /biography/Iamblichus.

72 *Lexico*, s.v. "Theurgy," accessed July 28, 2020, lexico.com/en/definition/theurgy.

73 *Encylopaedia Britannica*, "Iamblichus."

74 E. O. Wilson, "My Wish: Build the Encyclopedia of Life," *TED Talks*, March 2007, ted.com/talks/e_o_wilson _my_wish_build_the_encyclopedia_of _life/transcript.

75 Roland Wedlich-Söldner and Timo Betz, "Self-Organization: The Fundament of Cell Biology," *Philosophical Transactions of the Royal Society B* 373, no. 1747 (April 9, 2018), doi.org/10.1098 /rstb.2017.0103.

76 Stephen J. Martin et al., "A Vast 4,000-Year-Old Spatial Pattern of Termite Mounds," *Current Biology* 28, no. 22 (November 19, 2018), doi.org/10.1016 /j.cub.2018.09.061.

77 Lisa Margonnelli, "How Termites Shape the Natural World," *Scientific American*, August 1, 2018, doi.org/10.1038 /scientificamerican0818-74.

78 David Juliao, "Islamic Geometric Patterns: Religious Influences and Examples," *Study.com*, February 13, 2018, study.com/academy/lesson/islamic-geometric-patterns-religious-influences-examples.html.

79 A. K. Davidson, *The Art of Zen Gardens* (Los Angeles: Jeremy P. Tarcher, 1983), 25.

80 KCP International, "Haiku: Classic Japanese Poetry," accessed July 28, 2020, kcpinternational.com/2011/07 /haiku-classic-japanese-poetry.

81 Alfred Watkins, *The Old Straight Track: Its Mounds, Beacons, Moats, Sites, and Markstones* (London: Methuen, 1948), archive.org/details/b29827553/page/n7 /mode/2up.

82 Marilyn Walker, field notes, 2004.

83 Marilyn Walker, field notes, 2009.

84 Otgony Purev, *Mongolian Shamanism* (Ulaanbaatar: Authors Unlimited, 2005), 83.

85 Jennifer Ouellette, "A Math Theory for Why People Hallucinate," *Quanta Magazine*, July 30, 2018.

86 Hosch, *Britannica Guide to Geometry*.

87 Jnanamritananda, *Lead Us to the Light*.

88 Madhu Khanna, *Yantra: The Tantric Symbol of Cosmic Unity* (Rochester, VT: Inner Traditions, 2003).

89 Mata Amritanandamayi Math, "MA OM Meditation and Mantra Japa," *Amma's Talks*, September 23, 2018, amritayoga .com/yoga-talks/amma-talks/ma-om -meditation-and-mantra-japa/.

90 Pither, *Complete Book of Numbers*.

91 Karl Meninger, *Number Words and Number Symbols: A Cultural History of Numbers* (Cambridge, MA: MIT Press, 1970), 16.

92 Pither, *Complete Book of Numbers*, 5.

93 Keith Devlin, *The Millennium Problems: The Seven Greatest Unsolved Mathematical Puzzles of Our Times* (New York: Basic Books, 2002), 216.

94 Gordan R. Freeman, *Canada's Stonehenge: Astounding Archaeological Discoveries in Canada, England and Wales* (Cochrane, Alberta: Kingsley Publishing, 2009).

95 Ouellette, "A Math Theory for Why People Hallucinate."

96 Devlin, *Millennium Problems*, 180.

97 *BiologyOnline*, s.v. "Molecule," accessed July 28, 2020, biologyonline.com /dictionary/molecule.

98 *The Official Licensing Site of Albert Einstein*, accessed July 28, 2020, einstein.biz.

99 University of St. Andrews, Scotland, "Quotations: James Joseph Sylvester," *MacTutor*, accessed July 28, 2020, mathshistory.st-andrews.ac.uk /Biographies/Sylvester/quotations.

100 Livio, *Equation*, 21.

101 Paul Calter, "Pythagoras & Music of the Spheres," *Dartmouth College*, 1998, accessed July 28, 2020, math.dartmouth .edu/~matc/math5.geometry/unit3 /unit3.html.

102 Jane Bianksteen, "Computer Synthesizes 'Music of the Spheres,'" *New York Times*, April 24, 1979, nytimes.com/1979/04/24 /archives/computer-synthesizes-music -of-the-spheres-music-of-spheres.html.

103 Bianksteen, "Computer Synthesizes 'Music of the Spheres.'"

104 Albert-László Barabási and Eric Bonabeau, "Scale-Free Networks," *Scientific American*, May 2003, 60–69, doi .org/10.1038/scientificamerican0503-60.

105 Barabási and Bonabeau, "Scale-Free Networks."

106 Pither, *Complete Book of Numbers*, xi.

107 Hosch, *Britannica Guide to Geometry*.

108 Walker, "Circumpolar Shelter."

109 "Painting: Parabolic Triangles (Archimedes)," *National Museum of American History Behring Center*, accessed July 28, 2020, americanhistory.si.edu /collections/search/object/nmah_694655.

110 Hosch, *Britannica Guide to Geometry*.

111 Theodore A. Cook and Leonardo da Vinci, *The Curves of Life: Being an Account of Spiral Formations and Their Application to Growth in Nature, to Science, and to Art: with Special Reference to the Manuscripts of Leonardo da Vinci* (New York: Dover Publications, 1979).

112 "Plato, The Republic: 7. Book VII," *LiteraturePage.com*, accessed July 28, 2020, literaturepage.com/read/therepublic-272. html.

113 "Plato, The Republic: 7. Book VII," *LiteraturePage.com*.

114 Peter Lynch, "Quadrivium: The Noble Fourfold Way to an Understanding of the Universe," *The Irish Times*, July 20, 2017, irishtimes.com/news/science /quadrivium-the-noble-fourfold-way -to-an-understanding-of-the-universe -1.3153793#.XhyYK8v1H48.

115 Hosch, *Britannica Guide to Geometry*.

116 Hosch, *Britannica Guide to Geometry*.

117 Giannis Stamatellos, *Plotinus and the Presocratics: A Philosophical Study of Presocratic Influences in Plotinus' Enneads* (New York: State University of New York Press, 2007), 104.

118 James Luchte, *Pythagoras and the Doctrine of Transmigration* (New York: Bloomsbury Publishing, 2009), 172.

119 Lynch, "Quadrivium."

120 Carl Huffman, "Pythagoras," *The Stanford Encyclopedia of Philosophy*, ed. Edward N. Zalta (Winter 2018), plato.stanford.edu/entries/pythagoras.

121 "Pythagoras of Samos," *The Story of Mathematics*, accessed July 28, 2020, storyofmathematics.com/greek _pythagoras.html.

122 Lynch, "Quadrivium."

123 Lynch, "Quadrivium."

124 John A. Adam, *Mathematics in Nature: Modelling Patterns in the Natural World* (Princeton, NJ: Princeton University Press, 2003).

125 Marianne Freiberger, "Maths behind the Rainbow," *Plus*, October 21, 2011, plus.maths.org/content/rainbows.

126 Freiberger, "Maths behind the Rainbow."

127 Nibodhi Haas, *Rudraksha: Seeds of Compassion* (Kerala, India: Mata Amritanandamayi Mission Trust, 2013), 28.

128 Haas, *Rudraksha*, 101–102.

129 Marilyn Walker, "'Oh! You Mean You Have No Balance!' Symmetry, Science and Shamanism," in *Shamanhood and Mythology: Archaic Techniques of Ecstasy and Current Techniques of Research; In Honour of Mihály Hoppál, Celebrating His 75th Birthday* (Budapest: Hungarian Association for the Academic Study of Religions, 2017).

130 Livio, *Equation*.

131 Livio, *Equation*.

132 Miranda Lundy, *Sacred Geometry* (New York: Walker and Company, 1998), 45.

133 Marilyn Walker, "Symmetry, Science and Shamanism: Toward a 'Theory of Everything'?" *Cosmos* 24 (2010): 85–113.

134 Scott Olsen, *The Golden Section: Nature's Greatest Secret* (Wiltshire, England: Wooden Books, 2006).

135 Eliade, *Rights and Symbols*, x.

136 Stephen Skinner, *Sacred Geometry: Deciphering the Code* (New York: Sterling, 2006), 91.

137 Christopher Hitchens, "The Lovely Stones," *Vanity Fair*, July 2009, 44–47.

138 Wedlich-Söldner and Betz, "Self-Organization."

139 Marilyn Walker, "'Oh! You Mean You Have No Balance!'"; Walker, *Shamanism*.

140 Eliade, *Rights and Symbols*, x–xi.

141 Walker, *Shamanism*.

142 Kenneth G. Libbrecht, "Snowflake Science," *SnowCrystals.com*, accessed July 28, 2020, snowcrystals.com/science/science.html.

143 Oliver Moore, "The Science of Snowflakes," *The Globe and Mail*, January 23, 2013, theglobeandmail.com/news/national/the-science-of-snowflakes/article7735242.

144 S. W. Cranford et al., "Nonlinear Material Behaviour of Spider Silk Yields Robust Webs," *Nature* 482, no. 7383 (February 1, 2012): 72–76, doi.org/10.1038/nature10739.

145 Isabelle Su et al., "Imaging and Analysis of a Three-Dimensional Spider Web Architecture," *Journal of the Royal Society Interface* 15 (September 19, 2018), doi.org/10.1098/rsif.2018.0193.

146 Su et al., "Imaging."

147 Ball, *Patterns in Nature*, 80.

148 Ball, *Patterns in Nature*, 80.

149 Layal Liverpool, "Tiny Artificial Sunflowers Could Be Used to Harvest Solar Energy," *New Scientist*, November 4, 2019, newscientist.com/article/2222248-tiny-artificial-sunflowers-could-be-used-to-harvest-solar-energy/#ixzz6DlOLQwVD.

150 Skinner, *Sacred Geometry*.

151 Freeman, *Canada's Stonehenge*.

152 Ball, *Patterns in Nature*, 6.

153 Livio, *Equation*, 2.

154 Livio, *Equation*, 43–45.

155 Ball, *Patterns in Nature*, 14.

156 C. G. Jung, *The Collected Works of C.G. Jung, vol. 9: The Archetypes and the Collective Unconscious*, 2nd ed. (London: Routledge and Kegan Paul, 1969).

157 Robert A. Johnson, *We: Understanding the Psychology of Romantic Love* (San Francisco: Harper, 1983).

158 Jung, *Collected Works*, 33.

159 Johnson, *We*, 18–19.

160 Livio, *Equation*, 2.

161 Livio, *Equation*, 246.

162 Capra, *Tao of Physics*, 187.

163 "How Is Topology Applicable to the Real World?" video, *Institute for Advanced Study*, accessed July 28, 2020, ias.edu/ideas/2015/macpherson-topology-video.

164 Walker, *Shamanism*.

165 Walker, *Shamanism*.

166 Lynch, "Quadrivium."

167 Lundy, *Sacred Geometry*, 12.

168 Luigi Cocchiarella, ed., *ICGG 2018—Proceedings of the 18th International Conference on Geometry and Graphics: 40th Anniversary, Milan, Italy, August 3–7, 2018* (Berlin: Springer, 2019), 96.

169 "Solar Symmetry: Planets in Every Star System Form in the Same Shape Pattern," *Sputnik*, May 7, 2017, sputniknews.com/art_living/201707051055259051-planets-star-system-form.

170 Livio, *Equation*.

171 Pacioli, *De Divina Proportione*.

172 Puri, *Unforgettable Memories*.

173 Puri, *Unforgettable Memories*.

174 Joshua J. Mark, "The Vedas," *Ancient History Encyclopedia*, June 9, 2020, ancient.eu/The_Vedas.

175 Marshall Brain and Robert Lamb, "How Tornadoes Work," *HowStuffWorks*, accessed July 28, 2020, science.howstuffworks.com/nature/climate-weather/storms/tornado.htm.

176 Jeremy Shere, "What Are Solar Tornadoes?" *Moments of Science, Indiana Public Media*, July 19, 2012, indiana publicmedia.org/amomentofscience /solar-tornadoes.php.

177 "15.1: Structure of Water," in *15: Water*, LibreTexts libraries, last updated October 16, 2019, chem.libretexts.org /Bookshelves/Introductory_Chemistry /Book%3A_Introductory_Chemistry _(CK-12)/15%3A_Water/15.01%3A _Structure_of_Water.

178 D. L. Marrin, "Water and Nature's Geometry," *The Geometry of Nature*, May 2008, researchgate.net/publication/269693346 _Water_and_Nature's_Geometry.

179 Madhu Khanna, *Yantra: The Tantric Symbol of Cosmic Unity* (Rochester, VT: Inner Traditions, 2003).

180 Khanna, *Yantra*.

181 Khanna, *Yantra*, 6.

182 Galsan Tschinag, *The Blue Sky* (Lantzville, British Columbia, Canada: Oolichan Books, 2006).

183 Walker, "Circumpolar Shelter"; Walker, *Shamanism*.

184 R. Fletcher, "The Geometry of the Zodiac," *Nexus Network Journal* 11, no. 1 (April 2009), 105–28, doi.org/10.1007 /s00004-008-0106-x.

# INDEX

# PHOTO CREDITS

# ABOUT THE AUTHOR

**Marilyn Walker, PhD,** started her academic career as an archaeologist working in the Canadian North and then became involved in heritage preservation and museum curatorial work in Arctic and Subarctic Canada. Later, as a university professor of anthropology, her specialization in Indigenous studies, medical anthropology, and ethnobotany involved fieldwork across Canada and the United States and into Siberia, Mongolia, Southeast Asia, and India.

Personal and academic explorations in sacred geometry relate to her studies in shamanism and other spiritual traditions as well as in ethnomusicology and traditional medicine. She completed Michael Harner's three-year program at the Foundation for Shamanic Studies and was invited to become a field associate with the Foundation for Southeast Asia, Siberia, and Northern North America. A past member of the American Anthropological Association, the Society for the Anthropology of Religion, and the Explorers' Club, she has given papers and workshops nationally and internationally and authored scholarly and popular articles on shamanism, spirituality, traditional medicine, and music as well as two books on ethnobotany (*Harvesting the Northern Wild* and *Wild Plants of Eastern Canada*). Her most recent book is *Shamanism: An A–Z Reference Guide; Beliefs and Practices from around the World*. Her fieldwork, research, teaching, and publications on Indigenous cultures, shamanism, sacred geometry, music, and ethnobotany have been supported by the Russian Academy of Sciences, the Smithsonian Institution, the National Museums of Canada, and the Royal Ontario Museum as well as national and international funding agencies and institutions. Selected publications are available online and on her website, MarilynWalkerProductions.com.

She is especially interested in how sacred geometry offers new models of reality and consciousness and a renewed relationship with the natural world as well as a reconsidered life's purpose that could address the problems—personal and societal—of the modern world. It shows us who we truly are and points toward what we might become.

Dr. Walker is now professor emeritus at Mount Allison University in Canada. She retired to her long-term forest garden on Salt Spring Island, British Columbia, where she has a shamanic counseling practice and offers workshops on shamanism, drumming, energy medicine, and sacred geometry. She is also a visual artist and singer-songwriter who records and performs as Em Walker.